"What John shares with you in Win Today *is pure wisdom."*

—Jeffery J. Downs

Co-Author of *Streaking: The Simple Practice of Conscious, Consistent Actions that Create Life-Changing Results*

WIN TODAY

Embrace Discomfort, Look for Challenges, and **Win Every Day** with Small Daily Activities

John H. Fisher

Advantage | Books

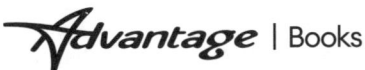

Copyright © 2023 by John H. Fisher.

All rights reserved. No part of this book may be used or reproduced in any manner whatsoever without prior written consent of the author, except as provided by the United States of America copyright law.

Published by Advantage, Charleston, South Carolina.
Member of Advantage Media.

ADVANTAGE is a registered trademark, and the Advantage colophon is a trademark of Advantage Media Group, Inc.

Printed in the United States of America.

10   9   8   7   6   5   4   3   2   1

ISBN: 978-1-64225-713-7 (Hardcover)
ISBN: 978-1-64225-712-0 (eBook)

LCCN: 2022920712

Cover design by Megan Elger.
Layout design by Wesley Strickland.

This publication is designed to provide accurate and authoritative information in regard to the subject matter covered. It is sold with the understanding that the publisher is not engaged in rendering legal, accounting, or other professional services. If legal advice or other expert assistance is required, the services of a competent professional person should be sought.

> Advantage Media helps busy entrepreneurs, CEOs, and leaders write and publish a book to grow their business and become the authority in their field. Advantage authors comprise an exclusive community of industry professionals, idea-makers, and thought leaders. Do you have a book idea or manuscript for consideration? We would love to hear from you at **AdvantageMedia.com**.

To my mom, Sally A. Fisher, for always making me feel like the most special person in the world

CONTENTS

Foreword xi

Introduction 1

PERSEVERANCE 7

Chapter 1: 9
How Dreams Come True

Chapter 2: 15
A Conversation That Changed My Life

Chapter 3: 21
A Story That Has to Be Told

Chapter 4: 27
The Story of an Aspiring Physician

EXECUTION 33

Chapter 5: 35
The Secret to Winning Today

Chapter 6: 45
How to Make Your Wildest Dreams Come True

HABITS 51

Chapter 7: 53
If I Die Today

Chapter 8: 65
Habits for a Happy Life

INTERPERSONAL SKILLS 79

Chapter 9: 81
How to Make Magical Things Happen

Chapter 10: 85
The Most Powerful Skills Your Children Need

Chapter 11: 93
The Scariest Day of My Life

HEALTH AND NUTRITION 99

Chapter 12: 101
How to Live a Long, Healthy Life

Chapter 13: 111
An (Almost) Guaranteed Way to Lose Weight

MENTAL HEALTH 119

Chapter 14: 121
The Journey of Self-Exploration

FINANCIAL MANAGEMENT 129

Chapter 15: 131
How You Can Become a Millionaire

FAITH 143

Chapter 16: 145
A Story of Hope

Chapter 17: 151
The Most Powerful Question You Will Ever Ask

Chapter 18: 157
An Open Letter to My Friend, an Atheist

Chapter 19: 165
What Would Jesus Do?

FAMILY 185

Chapter 20: 187
What It Means to Be Irish

Chapter 21: 193
Families Are Chosen, Not Born

PROFESSIONAL/GOAL SETTING 199

Chapter 22: 201
The Best Lesson a Father Can Give His Son

Chapter 23: 207
Why Lawsuits Matter

Chapter 24: 219
Three Simple Steps for Making Dreams Come True

Chapter 25: 225
Why Failure Is Essential to Success

SACRIFICE AND GENEROSITY 231
Chapter 26: 233
A Life Worthy of Respect

GRATITUDE AND LOVE 239
Chapter 27: 241
What It Means to Be a Friend
Chapter 28: 247
The Greatest Day of My Life
Conclusion: 251
Why Today Matters Most

FOREWORD

We learn through experience, either our own or others'. From others, we learn through reading, seeing, or hearing their stories. When you read a person's stories, you see who they are and what they have done to be who they are in life. It is rare to have someone write in a way so that you not only see who they are and who they are becoming but also learn what you can do to become who *you* want to be.

Today information is readily available. You can do a Google search on any word or topic and immediately have millions of answers from all kinds of sources. A good friend of mine says, "Information is cheap, but insights are invaluable." Information on its own only takes you so far, but when you get insights from a person who has applied that information—well, that is wisdom. When a person can give you wisdom, that is a gold vein in the mine of life.

What John shares with you in *Win Today* is pure wisdom. When you read and apply what he has written, you will have success in every area of life: personal, professional, physical, and spiritual. You will see how patience in small pursuits can yield big results. You will hear how life's challenges and struggles yield strength and perseverance.

You will feel the emotion of having your life's course changed in an instant and then the exhilaration of finding your life's calling. You will see how God, family, friends, and mentors can help you chart the right course rather than the course you thought you should be traveling.

Win Today is more than a title; it is a challenge and statement. It is a challenge to seek after and live a life that is giving and grateful. It is a challenge to be a net contributor rather than a net consumer. It is a challenge to tap into your inner fire and let it burn brightly for everyone to see.

It is a statement that everyone has within them the ability to win, that they can succeed at whatever they choose to do. It is a statement that your potential is unlimited. It is a statement that life is about accomplishing dreams and that whatever you dream is possible.

Warren Buffett, talking to a classroom of kids, gave them this analogy:

> *If I said to you I am going to give you a car, in fact, you can choose whatever car you want. Would you take me up on that deal? Now before you agree, here is the catch: it is the only car that you can ever own. You can only have this one car the rest of your life. If you took the deal, how would you treat that car? Would you take it in for regular maintenance? Would you make sure the oil was changed regularly? Would you wash it and shine it? Would you have insurance on it? If it were the only car you would ever have, then most likely you would do all those things and more. Now I want you to know that your body and your life are the only ones that you will ever have. So take care of it like you would if you only had one car.*

Win Today gives you what you need to care for your body and your life.

Keep smilin',

Jeffery J. Downs
Author, *Streaking: The Simple Practice of Conscious Consistent Actions That Make Life-Changing Results*

INTRODUCTION

The future depends on what you do today.
—**MAHATMA GANDHI**

Wherever you go, you will find people dreaming of a big future.

You will hear people tell you how they intend to conquer the world. And there's nothing wrong with big ambitions and even bigger dreams, but sadly in most cases, that's all they are: dreams. Talking about what you intend to achieve will not lead to the fulfillment of your dreams.

Success is made up of small moments of action—not day-to-day actions but moment to moment. What you are doing right now makes a difference, and the compound effect of your daily actions can lead to incredible results, both good and bad.

- If you want to have a great marriage with your spouse, give a sweet compliment to your spouse every day.

- If you want to lose weight, track your food consumption every day.

- If you want to build your relationship with your son, call or text him every day.

Where do you begin? Think of an activity that, if performed, would have a profound impact on your personal or professional life. This simple activity, while seemingly small, will have a profound influence on your life when done consistently every day. The results of simple daily activities—when done consistently—will amaze you.

Winning today doesn't have to be only a single activity. You can gradually create extraordinary results for your personal and professional life in many areas, but there's one catch: you need to *start today*. Stop waiting for the perfect time to begin exercising or dieting. The only right time to start is today.

> **You can gradually create extraordinary results for your personal and professional life in many areas, but there's one catch: you need to start today.**

And if you start now and win today with consistency, you will look back in three or four months with awe at how far you've come. Your dreams will begin to look realistic, and the cumulative results of simple daily activities will turn into results that you never thought possible.

Turns out, the key to success is winning today.

Why I Wrote This Book

Life is made up of small moments that make life special. These small moments happen at the most unexpected times and will be etched into your memory forever. It's not enough that you benefit from these special moments; you need to share them with the world.

That, my friend, is why I wrote this book. I want to unlock the memory bank and share with you the special experiences and lessons that have made a difference and that I hope can help you. The life experiences range from relationships with family and friends, faith, gratitude, and interpersonal skills to professional, financial, and health and fitness issues.

This book is my attempt to share those life experiences with you. In sharing these experiences, I hope you find that you are not alone—we all struggle with doubts, anxieties, and fears. I have made more than my share of mistakes and have had some epic failures along the way. But those mistakes and failures have made me who I am, and looking back, I wouldn't have it any other way.

Twelve Simple Virtues and Skills That Will Change Your Life

This book is broken down into twelve simple virtues and skills that can have the biggest impact on your life:

1. Perseverance
2. Execution
3. Habits
4. Interpersonal skills
5. Health and nutrition
6. Mental health
7. Financial management
8. Faith
9. Family
10. Professional and goal setting
11. Sacrifice and generosity
12. Gratitude and love

You may not agree with everything—and that's OK. Take what you can, tell me when I'm wrong, and keep fighting for the causes you were put on this earth for. And when you're finished reading, I hope you share the stories that have made the biggest impact on your life. Your friends and family deserve nothing less.

Thank you for taking this journey with me.

PERSEVERANCE

Our greatest weakness lies in giving up. The most certain way to succeed is always to try just one more time.
—THOMAS EDISON

CHAPTER 1:

HOW DREAMS COME TRUE

The news was not unexpected.

Sitting in the office of the assistant dean of the law school during an interview for admission to law school, I was told that my admission was a near impossibility. The assistant dean was breaking the bad news with kindness. I was told that my application was strong, but the law school had thirty-six hundred applicants for only 160 openings in the class. I could read between the lines—my application was not going to be accepted.

I expressed gratitude for our interview, and then I shared my story. From as early as I could remember, I only had one dream. Even as a child and young adult, I prayed for the chance to attend the only college I ever wanted to attend. I told the assistant dean that my dream had come true, and no one was going to take that away from me. The assistant dean listened to my story in silence and, after some thought, responded, "I had no idea you felt this way about Our Lady's University."

The assistant dean made a small compromise. The assistant dean explained that occasionally, for financial or family emergencies, some students did not return to school, and if that happened, he would give one of those spots to me. That was more than I could ask. But the first day of school was only seven weeks away, and I knew the odds were slim.

Three days before school was scheduled to begin, I took a flight to my dream school. If a spot opened for me, I wanted to be at the law school and ready to take it.

Two days before classes were to begin, I went to the assistant dean's office dressed in a suit and a tie at 8:00 a.m. I waited in the lobby of the assistant dean's office for 3.5 hours, waiting to meet with the assistant dean. Late in the morning, a receptionist told me that the assistant dean did not have time to meet with me. I was not completely surprised, as I did not have an appointment, so I left and told the receptionist that I would return the next morning.

One day before classes were scheduled to begin, I returned to the assistant dean's office at the law school. Again, I dressed to impress in a suit and tie and sat in the lobby of the assistant dean's office from 8:00 a.m. to 11:00 a.m. Later that morning, the receptionist told me that the assistant dean did not have time to meet with me. Frustrated that the assistant dean would not meet with me, I realized my admission to my dream law school was not going to happen. But again, I told the receptionist that I would return the next morning.

The next day was the first day of classes, and the law school was humming with the activity of students scurrying from class to class in the hallway. For the third consecutive day, I arrived at the assistant dean's office at 8:00 a.m. and waited in his lobby until the late morning.

After waiting for 3.5 hours, I accepted the reality that admission to my dream law school was not going to happen and pondered the thought of leaving. At that moment, I made a decision: I wasn't going anywhere until I had a meeting with the assistant dean. The assistant dean would have to give the bad news to me face to face, and I wasn't going anywhere until that happened.

At 11:35 a.m., the receptionist walked over to me and told me that the assistant dean would meet with me. Downtrodden and discouraged, I was ready for the bad news. I walked into the office of the assistant dean, shook his hand, and sat down. The assistant dean then told me something that I will never forget: "All of the students returned to school. We do not have an opening for you … but I'm going to open a spot for you anyway."

The assistant dean handed me an envelope that contained an acceptance letter to my dream school and told me to walk across the hallway, as my first class was about to begin. Stunned by what had just transpired, I left the assistant dean's office and walked into the classroom across from his office for my first class. That's how my first day began.

It would have been easy for me to give up, go home, and accept my second choice for a law school. But that would have meant giving up on my dream.

Dreams *can* come true. But you can't give up on your dreams, even when the odds seem impossible. Fight for your dreams. Never quit, and with some luck, your craziest, most impossible dreams might come true.

This is how dreams come true.

Dreams *can* come true. But you can't give up on your dreams, even when the odds seem impossible.

* * *

A Chance Worth Taking

On the morning of Election Day in 2014, my wife, Lisa, was dropping our boys off at their high school in Troy, New York. Just as our boys were about to get out of the car, Lisa asked them what they thought of her chances in the election for New York State Supreme Court Justice.

Our then-fourteen-year old son, Tim, responded, "It doesn't matter, Mom, whether you win or lose. You're a winner in my book." After our boys got out of the car, Lisa pulled over to the side of the road, and tears began flowing. Two months of pent-up emotions finally came to the surface. That is how Election Day began.

As she was a heavy underdog, I tried to get my wife ready for defeat on Election Day. I assured Lisa, "You'll be OK no matter what the result is, right?" and she responded, "I'll be fine … but I'm not going to lose." I did not have nearly as much confidence.

Truth is, it's not about winning or losing. Tim was right—regardless of the result, Lisa was a winner for taking a chance, even when the naysayers told her that victory was impossible.

Reflecting back, I know that dreams can come true. But even if Lisa had been defeated, she would have shown our children what it means to take a chance, fight hard for a dream, and ignore the naysayers. And in my view, that lesson is invaluable.

CHAPTER 2:

A CONVERSATION THAT CHANGED MY LIFE

Just a couple of weeks into my junior year at John A. Coleman High School in the fall of 1982, I was sitting at my desk in social studies class waiting for class to begin, when my teacher, Brother Armand, sat down across from me. With his face just a couple of feet away from mine, Brother Armand bluntly told me, "You are a loser, and you'll always be a loser."

Not a great way to start the day and more than just a little disturbing. But then Brother Armand explained, "You have more ability than anyone in this class, but you don't give any effort. I'll make a deal with you: if you give your best effort for our first exam and don't do well, I'll never ask you to study hard again, and I'll leave you alone." Fair enough, and I quickly agreed ... but of course, I had no intention of studying for the exam.

An Epiphany for Yours Truly

On the night before the exam, I was sitting in my bedroom reading sports magazines (while I was supposed to be studying), and I was bored silly. With nothing else to do, I picked up my social studies book and read it for a couple of hours. This was far from my best effort, but it was still more studying than I had ever done for an exam.

On the day after the social studies exam, Brother Armand dropped the exam paper on my desk as he handed them out. My exam paper read at the top: A-. I was stunned. I had been a C and B student all my life, and I didn't know what an A was. *Was this some kind of cruel joke?* I thought. *How can this be?* My friends and classmates had always told me that I was "stupid," and I assumed they were right.

Later that afternoon I bumped into Brother Armand outside the front entrance of my high school. As he walked by me on the front steps of Coleman High School, Brother Armand looked at me and said something that I will never forget: "This is just the beginning for you." I still thought he was nuts, but just maybe he was onto something.

A Shocking Result That No One Could Predict

A week later I had my first exam in the most difficult subject area: French III. I hated French in my first two years of high school, and it showed in my grades. I had been a C and D student in my first two years of French, and now I was on the verge of taking an advanced French class in a class full of straight-A honors students. I was horribly unprepared to begin French III, and my teacher was prepared to write me off.

Just before the first exam, my French teacher gave me an ultimatum: if I didn't pass the exam, she would kick me out of her class. Ouch! I decided at that moment that I was going to prove her wrong, and for the first time in my life, I studied for the exam with a passion. On the night before the exam, I stayed up until 1:00 a.m. studying until I couldn't hold my eyes open, but even with my hard work, I had no idea if I could pass the exam. I knew the odds were still stacked against me.

On the day after I took the French exam, my French teacher stood at the front of the classroom and told the class, "The top score on the exam is John Henry Fisher with a ninety-six." I was dumbfounded. This couldn't be right—this class was loaded with the top students in the school, and I had just beat all of them?

It dawned on me at that moment. My friends and classmates were wrong—I wasn't stupid. OK, I knew I wasn't a Rhodes scholar, but for the first time in my young life, I realized that I wasn't dumb either. But more importantly, I discovered that when I gave my best effort, I could beat almost anyone.

> **I discovered that when I gave my best effort, I could beat almost anyone.**

How My Life Was Changed Inside Out

From that moment, I worked with a passion. Any goofing off was now taboo, and I gave the same effort in my other subjects that I had given on the French III exam. I was no longer the class clown or the life of the party, but I was determined and laser focused on my studies ... and my world changed almost overnight. I finished the fall semester with one of the highest GPAs in my class, and as hard as it was to believe for everyone (except Brother Armand), I was now in the high honors of my class.

I never looked back. I now had a formula for success that couldn't be beat—I knew that If I outworked my competition, I could not only compete with my peers, but I could beat them every time. And the results were shocking: I finished my first year of college in the top 3 percent of my class. And I went on to do well at one of the top colleges and law schools in the country.

A Little Note of Gratitude for Changing My Life

I now realize that I will never be the brightest person in the courtroom, and there will always be other lawyers with more intelligence and credentials than me, *but no one will outwork me*. And I never would have discovered this without the not-so-subtle challenge from Brother Armand in the fall of 1982. It just took one person to believe in me.

Among the special gifts in my life (which are many), I can't think of any that are better. Thank you, Brother Armand and John A. Coleman High School, for changing my life.

CHAPTER 3:

A STORY THAT HAS TO BE TOLD

A quick explanation for why this story was written. In sharing this story, my intention is not to disparage my father. I deeply love my father and appreciate and value the sacrifices that he made for my family and me. My father made me who I am.

Like every person, my father was not perfect. I am sharing one particular imperfection for the children—young and old—of alcoholic parents. I want you to know that your experience is not unique, and you are not alone. I hope sharing my story will help you overcome any feelings of guilt and shame that you may have today, even (for some of you) many years after your childhood.

This is why I feel compelled to share this story. Although my father is not alive today, my hope is that he would understand that this is a story that needs to be told.

* * *

Not Your Typical Meeting

This wasn't your typical meeting. My mother, my three sisters, and I were meeting to discuss, for the first time, a plan for challenging my father into sobriety … and the meeting was long overdue. Alcoholism has many victims—family members who are witnesses to the devastating toll that the disease takes on the alcoholic and the less obvious damage that it has upon the alcoholic's spouse and children.

Finally, after twenty-plus years, enough was enough. This meeting was a last-ditch effort to save my dad (and perhaps save our family) from the ravages of alcoholism that refused to ease their grip on him. Years of my dad going to Alcoholics Anonymous meetings seemed to accomplish little, and our pleas to get help fell on deaf ears. Dad seemingly felt comfortable with the status quo, and we knew an intervention had almost no chance.

A Shocking Epiphany

But on a wing and a prayer, my mom, my three sisters, and I took a chance. An intervention with an alcoholic takes planning, and the preintervention meetings with an addiction counselor focused on the impact that our dad's alcoholism had upon each of us. When my turn came, I shared with the group—for the first time—a feeling that I had since my childhood: that I was the one to blame for my dad's drinking.

The counselor nodded his head in understanding and, in a matter-of-fact way, responded that it is common for children of alcoholic parents to blame themselves. Children of alcoholic parents assume they are the cause of their parents' alcoholism. In fact, I was told, it would be uncommon for the child of an alcoholic parent to think otherwise.

I looked down at the floor in disbelief as I began to question whether my lifelong assumption was true. Hard to believe after years of accepting blame for my dad's drinking, but I began to think that maybe I was not at fault. The logic made sense—my dad's drinking was a choice that he made, and my mother, my sisters, and I were powerless to stop it. We were simply witnesses to a horrible addiction.

Words of gratitude wouldn't be enough. For the first time, I knew that I had done nothing wrong. I could not have stopped my dad from having a drink, and with the power that alcohol had on him, he had almost no control. Even if the intervention did not stop my dad's drinking, I left the meeting that night knowing that years of guilt were lifted from my shoulders.

A Coping Mechanism That Didn't Work

The counselor told us that families create coping mechanisms to ease the burden of having an alcoholic parent. And in our family's case, our coping mechanism was to deny that Dad's alcoholism had any effect on our lives. My mother, my sisters, and I simply pretended as though the problem did not exist.

Denying my dad's drinking problem could not always be avoided. Every so often, I would find my father passed out on the couch in our living room, and I would carry his lifeless body over my shoulders to his bedroom. But most of the time, my dad could take care of himself and only wanted my sisters, mother, and me to avoid telling him what to do.

None of us had the slightest clue of the impact that my dad's drinking had upon us. I applied the coping mechanism to every relationship in my life—no one could hurt me if I didn't get close to them. My relationships were superficial, and I cannot think of a single occasion that I expressed genuine weakness or vulnerability with anyone.

The Hidden Impact of Alcoholism

The results were predictable. At age twenty-five, I was a closed book with the inability to express genuine emotions or feelings. Just like my dad, I didn't want to change my ways, and I knew that no one could hurt me if I didn't let them see who I was. Life was OK, I thought at the time, but I now realize it never really was.

In the days leading up to the intervention, it occurred to me that my way of coping through denial could change. I was just beginning to understand the impact of alcoholism and how it affected my relationships and my inability to share feelings and emotions. If I could just share a few of these feelings with my dad, maybe I could make a change.

An Intervention That Changed My Life

On the afternoon of the intervention, my expectations were low. I knew my dad would resist treatment for alcoholism and might not even stay in the room to listen. Each of us, in turn, told my dad about our experiences with his alcoholism and how it made us feel. My dad listened stoically.

> **In just a few minutes, I unleashed pent-up anger from years of hidden emotion ... and it felt damn good.**

When my turn came, I turned to the only emotion I had at that moment: anger. If Dad would not go for treatment right now, I would not forgive him. This was, I told him, a small favor to ask, and I needed an answer right now. In just a few minutes, I unleashed pent-up anger from years of hidden emotion ... and it felt damn good.

At the end of the intervention, my dad asked if he could leave and promised to someday get treatment. Sadly that day never came. My dad died at age seventy in January, 2005.

A Story with a Happy Ending

To this day, my mother and sisters tell me the intervention was a failure—we didn't accomplish anything because Dad didn't stop drinking. In my view, they are wrong. While the intervention didn't stop my dad's drinking, it changed my life. I understood, for the first time in my twenty-five years, that I no longer had to bear the guilt for my dad's drinking, and it was OK to share my feelings and every so often get hurt.

Within months of the intervention, I met my future wife. For the first time in my life, I began sharing little bits of my feelings and thoughts with Lisa, and to my surprise, she didn't laugh at me. *Things just might be OK*, I thought. Turns out, things are great—Lisa and I will celebrate twenty-eight years of marriage in 2023, and I count her love for me as one of the greatest blessings in my life.

I was tempted to keep this story locked away or share it with only a few family members or friends, but I knew that wouldn't be right. If you know a child of an alcoholic parent, you might consider sharing my story with them.

CHAPTER 4:

THE STORY OF AN ASPIRING PHYSICIAN

"You're too old for medical school." Those were the discouraging words that the thirty-four-year-old aspiring physician was told by the dean of students at his college. The dean of students refused to give a recommendation for the aspiring physician's application for medical school.

When he shared his plans to apply to medical school, the aspiring physician's friends told him that it was impossible and scoffed at his dream: "Do you realize how hard it is to be accepted at medical school?"

The aspiring physician thought, *What do I have to lose?* In the worst case, the aspiring physician would be rejected by all three medical schools to which he applied. The aspiring physician thought, *Why not try?*

The aspiring physician applied to and was accepted by all three medical schools.

A Path Less Traveled

The first year of medical school is so difficult that it breaks the resolve of even the brightest medical students. Many students quit in their first year.

During his medical residency, the aspiring physician worked twenty-four-hour shifts and late nights at the hospital to put food on the table for his wife and daughter. Often sleep deprived, the aspiring physician just kept working.

In his early forties, "Dr. Bill"—as he was now known—became an anesthesiologist, but he was much more than a physician. Whenever an anesthesiologist was needed at the hospital at 2:00 a.m., other physicians knew that Dr. Bill would always be the first to get out of bed and rush to the hospital. Dr. Bill always put the needs of his patients first.

The Birth of an American Dream

This American Dream was born in a small factory town in northwest Connecticut.

The dreamer had little in the way of opportunity. His parents worked in a factory, and his siblings would work there too. The dreamer appeared destined to spend his life working in a small factory town doing what his parents had done.

While working as a volunteer firefighter, the dreamer saw the work of paramedics, and it dawned on him that perhaps he could do the same thing. So the dreamer went to college and took classes to become a paramedic.

While working as a paramedic, the dreamer saw the work of physicians and thought that perhaps he could do the same. So the dreamer studied hard and got top grades in order to pursue his dream of becoming a physician.

Day by day, the dreamer moved in the direction of his dreams and did not listen to the naysayers. Eventually, after facing down the naysayers and overcoming one seemingly insurmountable obstacle after the next, the dreamer achieved his dream.

The Truth about the American Dream

The American dream is not born in affluent neighborhoods or prestigious universities. That is a myth. The American dream is born in the heart of a dreamer who sees opportunities and fights to protect his dream. And in the case of Dr. Bill, the American dream was born in perhaps the least expected place: a small factory town in northwest Connecticut.

The best gift you can give your children is to give them an example of how to live life. And in some cases, this means fighting for your dreams and refusing to listen when others try to tell you that your dream is impossible.

There is no better example of the American dream than Dr. Bill, but he was much more than a dreamer. Dr. Bill worked hard, faced obstacles at every twist in the road, and refused to give up on his dream.

> **The best gift you can give your children is to give them an example of how to live life.**

And I am so proud to call Dr. Bill my father-in-law. Dr. Bill's daughter (my wife, Lisa) and our three children could not have a better role model for living a life of integrity, hard work, and determination to pursue a dream at all costs.

I am grateful to have a father-in-law who personifies the American dream.

PS: My father-in-law passed from this world into God's hands on June 13, 2022. I miss him every day. God bless this great man.

* * *

The Purpose of Life

When you look back on your life, it won't matter what car you drive or how big your house is. Those things are meaningless.

What makes life special is the impact that you've had on the lives of others. Specifically what you've done to help others—but not just your family members. What have you done for complete strangers who had nothing to give you? That's where sacrifice and generosity are defined.

My father-in-law, Bill, defined his life by generosity and sacrifice for those who need it the most. In a world where success tends to be defined by material abundance, Bill defied conventional notions of wealth through sacrifice and dedication to those he served as a physician.

These are stories that will never be told. Why? Because Bill did not sacrifice for his patients for the sake of notoriety or money—he made sacrifices out of compassion, generosity, and love. By living a life of sacrifice for the less fortunate, Dr. Bill set the perfect example for his family, and for all who have known him, our lives have been blessed.

Bill showed us how to live a life of purpose by the example of his life. God bless Bill Hodorski for showing us the real meaning of life.

William R. Hodorski, DO (August 29, 1953–June 13, 2022)

EXECUTION

When you improve conditioning a little each day, eventually you have a big improvement in conditioning. Not tomorrow, not the next day, but eventually a big gain is made. Don't look for the big, quick improvement. Seek the small improvement one day at a time. That's the only way it happens.

When you improve a little each day, eventually big things occur and when it happens, it lasts.

—JOHN WOODEN

CHAPTER 5:

THE SECRET TO WINNING TODAY

Many business owners search for the secret that will launch them into instant success and highly profitable businesses. These people jump around from one marketing gimmick to the next in a continual search for the one thing that will lead to a thriving business. No one told these business owners that the magical fairy dust doesn't exist (or they weren't listening).

But there is a secret to success, and it doesn't involve a marketing gimmick. This one thing is done by very few, but for those who do, it almost always brings long-term success. It is simply this: *consistency in a single daily activity*. Specifically, doing small activities *every day* that will have a profound influence on your career and personal life.

The concepts are derived from the amazing book *Streaking: The Simple Practice of Conscious, Consistent Actions that Create Life-Changing Results*, coauthored by Jeffery J. Downs, a practice leader of FranklinCovey and a consultant for leading Fortune 500 companies.

The Secret to Changing Your Life and Career

The basic premise is that excellence in professional or personal pursuits—is determined by one thing: consistency. The elite performers (e.g., Warren Buffett) do remarkably simple activities but are highly consistent and do not deviate from them, not even for a single day. Without question, consistency is the signature trait of highly successful people.

> **Excellence—in professional or personal pursuits—is determined by one thing: consistency.**

Comedian Jerry Seinfeld will tell you that the key to his success was writing at least one joke every day. Writing a single joke only took a few minutes a day, but with time and patience, Seinfeld had thousands of jokes. Author and thought leader Seth Godin has written a blog post every day for over eleven years. Hall of Fame shortstop Cal Ripken played in every game (2,632 games) for over sixteen years. The results of their consistency are mind boggling.

Consistency in doing a small thing over time will yield awesome results.
—JEFFERY J. DOWNS AND JAMI L. DOWNS,
Streaking: The Simple Practice of Conscious, Consistent Actions That Create Life-Changing Results

What do you need to do that—if you did it every day—would make the biggest impact on your professional and personal life? The activity might take five to ten minutes (or less), but over time, the cumulative impact of doing the activity *every day* will profoundly impact your career and life. Simply put, there is nothing that will influence your long-term success more than streaking.

How to Change Your Career and Life by Streaking

Streaking can be done in three simple steps:

STEP 1: IDENTIFY A LAUGHABLY SIMPLE ACTIVITY

Pick an activity that is "laughably simple" to do. The activity is so simple that you would be crazy not to do it. This activity will, over time, have a profound impact on your professional or personal life. It is amazing what you can achieve when you do one "laughably simple" activity every day.

- If you want better fitness, commit to jogging *at least* one mile every day.
- If you want to write a book, commit to writing *at least* one sentence every day.
- If you want to get more Google reviews for your business, commit to requesting *at least* one Google review on a daily basis.
- If you want to improve your marriage, commit to saying one nice thing to your spouse *at least* once a day.
- If you want to learn a foreign language, commit to learning a new word or phrase *at least* once a day.
- If you want a stronger relationship with your college-aged son, commit to calling him *at least* once a day.

There's no limit to what you can achieve when you're streaking. Notice the inclusion of the words "at least" in each activity. You are free to do more if you choose, but at a bare minimum, you will do *at least* what you say you will do. You may want to jog two to three miles, but every day, you will jog at least one mile.

STEP 2: DOCUMENT YOUR STREAK IN A JOURNAL

The record or journal is the physical manifestation of your streak. Every day, document what you've done and tally the results of your streak (e.g., "Day 412 of streak: Total distance jogged 1,075 miles"). Over time, you can reflect back by reviewing your journal and appreciate how far you've gone.

> *Without a record, you don't have a streak.*
> **—JEFFERY J. DOWNS AND JAMI L. DOWNS,**
> Streaking: The Simple Practice of Conscious, Consistent Actions That Create Life-Changing Results

If you miss a day and break your streak, you can begin a new streak. But ideally you will keep the streak going at all costs.

STEP 3: SHARE YOUR SUCCESS AND RESULTS WITH A STREAKING COMMUNITY

Don't do this alone—that is a recipe for failure. Join a community of like-minded streakers, and share your results on a daily basis. The community of streakers will encourage and inspire you when you don't want to keep going.

It's rare for streaks to exist outside community.
—JEFFERY J. DOWNS AND JAMI L. DOWNS,
Streaking: The Simple Practice of Conscious, Consistent Actions That Create Life-Changing Results

Share your journal entries with your streaking community. Tally the results for your fellow streakers, and take some pride in your results. You are on your way to greatness.

Why Streaking Works

The biggest problem that you face is just getting started. You know you should exercise more or call your son more often, but you're busy, and somehow things always seem to get in the way. It's as though life is conspiring against your most important priorities.

That's why making your activity "laughably simple" is crucial. The activity should not be difficult to do because if it is too challenging, your streak won't last. You're free to challenge yourself to achieve more, but your streak must be based on an activity that you would be crazy not to do.

The success of keeping the streak alive will pay massive compound interest.
—JEFFERY J. DOWNS AND JAMI L. DOWNS,
Streaking: The Simple Practice of Conscious, Consistent Actions That Create Life-Changing Results

Once your streak builds momentum, you will find a groove and want to keep it going at all costs. Authors Jeffery J. Downs and his wife, Jami L. Downs, have jogged at least one mile every day (they take

Sundays off) for over six years, and the results? Excellent fitness and health—and a stronger marriage. The impact at first might not seem like much, but over time, the cumulative results of streaking are awesome.

The Powerful Impact of Streaking

Streaking can be an activity that you do daily, weekly, or monthly.

Monthly. Our law firm has sent a print newsletter, *Lawyer Alert*, to our referral partners every month for over eleven years. The monthly print newsletters are ideal for staying top of mind with your referral partners. The results? Our firm has increased the number of our referral partners from 124 to 532. That, my friend, is the power of a conscious, deliberate action done every month.

Weekly. St. Louis attorneys Tyson Mutrux, Esq., and Jim Hacking, Esq., host a fantastic lawyer podcast, the *Maximum Lawyer*, with new guests every week. Entertaining and full of valuable information, the *Maximum Lawyer* podcast has evolved into something even greater, with a thriving Facebook group of almost 5,000 lawyers.

Tyson and Jim will tell you that *consistency* is the secret to their podcast's success. Every week without fail, Tyson and Jim record a new podcast, and they've been doing this for years. Yes, streaking is the key to the success of the *Maximum Lawyer* podcast.

Daily. For the past 570 days, I've jogged at least one mile every day. It might not seem like much to jog as little as one or two miles on most days, but over the course of 570 days, I've jogged 1,476 miles (the equivalent of more than fifty-six marathons).

Over the course of a little more than one year, I documented my food consumption and exercise on a daily basis with MyBodyTutor.com (highly recommended!). Based upon this conscious and intentional action, my body weight dropped from 193.6 lbs. to 165.6 lbs. This didn't happen overnight. I only lost about half a pound a week, but over the course of a little more than one year, the consistency of this daily habit resulted in a weight loss of twenty-eight pounds.

It might not seem like much when you're streaking, but when you tally the results, you appreciate the pretty incredible results of streaking.

The Power of a "Be Statement"

To go one step further, create an affirmative statement of who you want to be, and write this statement in your journal every day. This affirmative "be statement" of your identity will help you become the person you are striving to become.

> *A simple statement of affirmation about who you want to be, noted daily, will positively change your life.*
> **—JEFFERY J. DOWNS AND JAMI L. DOWNS,**
> Streaking: The Simple Practice of Conscious, Consistent Actions That Create Life-Changing Results

The affirmative identity statement is a statement of aspiration of who you want to become (e.g., "I want to be a marathon runner" or "I want to be the lawyer with the most Google reviews in New York"). By writing the affirmative "be statement" every day in your streaking journal, you will continually reinforce your desired identity.

How to Begin Streaking

Just start streaking today. Do the one thing that, over time, will have a profound influence on your life or career. Document your streak in a journal, and you're streaking, baby!

> **Do the one thing that, over time, will have a profound influence on your life or career.**

Read Jeffery J. Downs and Jami L. Downs's book, *Streaking: The Simple Practice of Conscious, Consistent Actions That Create Life-Changing Results*—it is a quick read and can have a powerful impact for you. Jeff and Jami also have a podcast, *Streaking* (StreakingMastery.com/podcast), and a free app, StreakingMastery.com.

Dream big. Start small. But most of all, start.
—SIMON SINEK

Don't streak alone. We have a small community of like-minded streakers in a private Facebook group (The Streakers). Why not join the fun? Send an email to jfisherlawyer@gmail.com with the subject line "I want to streak," and I will be happy to add you to our streaking community.

Streaking Puts Time on Your Side

When you streak, your results build over time into something amazing. When you are streaking, time is working *for* you, not against you.

Streaking can help you accomplish the wildest goals in your life and career. Months, and maybe years, after you begin your streak, you will look back and marvel at how far you've gone. Streaking is how elite performers succeed at life and business, and there's no reason you can't streak with them.

CHAPTER 6:

HOW TO MAKE YOUR WILDEST DREAMS COME TRUE

All your life people tend to tell you what you can't do. Even your parents may have told you that your dreams were unrealistic and you had to "get your head out of the clouds." But what if anything truly is possible? What if there is no limit to the possibilities, and even your most outrageous dreams somehow become possible?

Dreams are what make life worth living. But if you don't fulfill your dreams, they have no value. So, what can you do to make your wildest dreams come true?

Four Steps to Becoming a Dream Maker
STEP 1: THE DREAM BOOK

A dream has to live in language—you have to give it words. Once you give the dream words, it has power. Allow yourself to imagine and write a list of dreams that brings them to the surface. Identify the dreams that you have courage to do, and take a little action. What is the future, and where do you want to go?

> **A dream has to live in language—you have to give it words. Once you give the dream words, it has power.**

Just writing a dream can have a powerful effect on your ability to accomplish it.

—**DAN RALPHS,** *Dream Leadership Consulting*

Spend a day in the imagination state with no electronics or interruptions. Make a list of your one hundred biggest dreams. Just write down your dreams without committing to them. Always think of the "and" rather than the "or." If you need help, go to Bucketlist.org for a list of dreams.

Your dreams my fall into one of twelve categories:

- Physical: Lifestyle habits, addictions, exercise
- Emotional: Relationships, security, helping others
- Intellectual: Reading, learning, continuous improvement tasks
- Spiritual: Peace with yourself, learning the scriptures
- Psychological: Overcome fears and insecurities, develop willpower
- Material: Own a home, own a Tesla
- Professional: A promotion, a new product/service, sales/income goals
- Financial: Freedom from debt, investment goals, financial freedom
- Creative: Explore the arts, write a book

- Adventure: Mountain climbing, exotic holidays, scuba diving
- Legacy: Instill values in your children, volunteer, charitably give, save the world
- Character: Develop patience, walk the talk, earn respect, be worthy of trust

Next to each dream in your Dream Book, enter the date that you wrote the dream and when you plan to achieve it. The duration of a dream can be short term (ST): less than one year; moderate term (MT): one to five years; or long term (LT): more than five years. When you achieve a dream, mark the date in your Dream Book, and add bigger dreams.

Glance through your Dream Book for a few moments every day just as a reminder of your dreams. You will grow into a much different person as you begin to pursue your dreams. Those who have accomplished dreams are far more generous than those who haven't.

2: THE DREAM MANAGER

The Dream Manager will help in articulating your dreams and formulating a plan for achieving your dreams. The Dream Manager might help you design a savings plan and assess your financial situation.

> *Don't ever let someone tell you, you can't do something. You got a dream, you gotta protect it. When people can't do something themselves, they're gonna tell you that you can't do it. You want something, go get it. Period.*
> **—WILL SMITH** *in The Pursuit of Happiness*

The Dream Manager's role will be to listen without judgment and encourage and inspire you to pursue your dreams. Over time, your trusted friend may begin sharing their dreams with you. You will have regular "dream sessions" with your trusted advisor, and their role is to guide you in the direction of your dreams.

STEP 3: THE DREAM SESSION

You might meet with your Dream Manager for thirty minutes once a month to discuss your future and dreams. You may want to add more ambitious dreams to the list during the monthly dream sessions.

> *Just talking about our dreams moves us in the direction of them.*
> —**MATTHEW KELLY,** *The Dream Manager*

Focus on one dream that you can accomplish in the next twelve to eighteen months. Your spouse and children may want to join in the Dream Sessions, and you might encourage them to have their own Dream Books.

Don't be shy about talking to others about your dreams. There is nothing more powerful than sharing your dreams with others and asking them to hold you accountable.

STEP 4: THE DREAM WALL

Write your dreams on a whiteboard/wall (a.k.a. the Dream Wall). As dreams are fulfilled, cross them off the Dream Wall, and celebrate and have a party. Share with others that you're living a dream.

> *Dreams are the core of every person. It is there that our passion for life is ignited.*
> —**MATTHEW KELLY,** *The Dream Manager*

What are your excuses for not pursuing your dreams? For most people, the excuses are the lack of time and money. So what can you do about this? Make more money, and create more time. How much money do you need to live your wildest dream? Once you know what that number is, you can work to make it happen.

There are just two questions for you: What's your dream? And why aren't you living it?

HABITS

Success consists of going from failure to failure without loss of enthusiasm.

—WINSTON CHURCHILL

CHAPTER 7:

IF I DIE TODAY

If I die today, I want you to be happy. If I've lived my life the right way, I will be with God, and nothing could make me happier. Know that I am at peace.

You can honor my life by living your life with enthusiasm and passion. Do not worry about me—I am in a better place. Make your life amazing.

Seventeen Steps for Living a Better Life

These are the principles that have served me well. Take them for what they are worth, and perhaps reread them from time to time when you are feeling down.

1. **Live for the moment.** There is no magical destination where life will be perfect. That is a myth. The beauty of life is in the journey. Savor the journey. Treat every moment as if it is precious, because it is.

2. **Dream without limitation.** Nothing is impossible. Write down your wildest, craziest dreams in a journal, and reread the journal from time to time. Don't let anyone tell you that you can't achieve your dreams.

   > *The greater danger for most of us is not that our aim is too high and we miss it, but that it is too low and we reach it.*
   > **—MICHELANGELO**

3. **Make mistakes—lots of them.** Those who make mistakes are the most successful. Do not be afraid of mistakes—embrace them.

   > *I've missed more than 9,000 shots in my career. I've lost almost 300 games. Twenty-six times, I've been trusted to take the game winning shot and missed. I've failed over and over and over again in my life. And that is why I succeed.*
   > **—MICHAEL JORDAN**

4. **Become the best version of yourself.** Whenever you have a decision to make throughout the course of a day, ask, "Will this make me a better version of myself?" If so, do it. Asking this question is a fulcrum for all of life's decisions.

5. **Your word is everything.** Without integrity and honesty, you have no chance. Your word is your most precious asset. Live a life of uncompromising integrity.

6. **Everyone is your equal.** Regardless of who they are, everyone is a child of God and should be treated as your equal.

7. **Hang out with the winners.** Make friends with those who are the highest achievers. You will be the average of the five persons you spend the most time with. Don't waste time with the lazy and unmotivated.

8. **Outwork your peers.** Hard work beats talent. The smartest and most intelligent never beat the hard workers. Work harder than your peers, and you will beat them every time. Work like your life depends on it—because it does.

> **Hard work beats talent. The smartest and most intelligent never beat the hard workers.**

9. **Work on your relationships.** The value of life comes from your relationships. Spend time every day nurturing your friendships and relationships, and you will be rich.

10. **Possessions mean nothing.** Do not spend your time obsessed over possessions. Possessions will not make you happy. Happiness is derived from incredible experiences and serving others.

11. **Find your passion.** Find a field of work that you love. When you are passionate about what you do, work becomes fun.

12. **Don't quit.** Failure is impossible for those who refuse to quit. When you are focused on a goal and refuse to quit, success is inevitable.

13. **Spend time with God.** Nurture your relationship with God through prayer. Spend time every day in the classroom of silence with God. God wants nothing more than your time.

14. **Do not dwell on the past.** Everyone makes mistakes and has done things that they're not proud about. Forget about the past, and focus on making small, incremental improvements in your life every day.

15. **Forgive without limitation.** Forgive without reservation, and do not hold grudges. Your resentment and grudges will only hurt you.

16. **Never stop learning.** Be a continual learner. Read every day, and strive to learn something new. Reading is the greatest skill a person can have.

17. **Exercise every day.** Never let a day go by without exercise, even if it is twenty-five push-ups or a half-mile jog. Treat your body like you will live forever. Your body will reward you when you get older.

The life you create is in your hands—I only ask that you do your best.

* * *

Words of Wisdom from Dad

When I was a junior in high school, my father, James H. Fisher, Esq., wrote an eleven-page letter intended as a road map for my future. The words were written with a pen and paper, but they might as well have been written in granite.

I cherish my dad's letter and reread it whenever I need reinforcement of the most important principles to living a successful life. I hope these words help you.

- **Life itself is a lesson.**

- "There's never a day that goes by, no matter how old we are, that we don't learn something new and draw some lesson from just plain daily living. I'm talking of the lessons of life—not formal education."
- "Those who accept and benefit from the lessons of life are the people we call 'mature' … even bad things and disappointments can be good things if we learn from them."

- **Hard, unrelenting work is the most important thing.**
  - "Please don't get the idea that I am asking you to be a high achiever for me and your mother. I'm not. I'm asking you to do it for *you* and to be mindful of its importance."
  - "It means *hard, unrelenting* work, but it will pay great dividends. By striving to achieve now, you will develop a pattern and personality that will become part of your adult life. It is the single, important thing that other people, and especially prospective employers, will look for and respect."

- **Failure is part of life.**
  - "You must be mindful that failures and disappointments are part of life. Everyone has them in varying degrees. But it is the strong, mature person who copes with setbacks, puts them behind and uses them as a motivation to overcome—to strive harder."
  - "You may have heard it said that God operates in mysterious ways and that things happen for the best, or out of

bad things and disappointments always come something good. We should look at it that way."

- **Set your goals high.**
  - "A teacher once said to me in words or substance: we don't expect you to accomplish the impossible. You should not fall apart over failure, *provided* you gave it your best shot."
  - "Picture a bull's-eye (target), and you are holding the bow and arrow. If you aim for the center of the target (bull's-eye), you may miss, but it's more likely you'll come close to it. On the other hand, if you just aim to hit the overall target, rather than the center of it, you may miss the entire thing."
  - "The obvious point is that if you strive for perfection, the more likely it is that you will achieve it or come close. If you don't set your aims high, the greater chance for failure."

- **Be a leader.**
  - "Be as friendly as you can, and *be humble*. Never try to act like a wise guy or hotshot. It never pays."
  - "But at the same time, be your own man. Stand on your own two feet. Strive to be a leader and not a follower. Don't look up to people, but at the same time, don't look down on them."

- **Treat everyone as your equal.**
  - "Remember that everyone is a human being and has emotions. Everyone wants to be liked and well thought of, even if they don't show it."

- "Never treat anyone like a lesser human being because he or she has no education, a lowly job, a handicap, or an abrasive personality—they usually can't help it."

- **Stick with the winners.**
  - "A key thing to remember throughout your life is to *stick with the winners.*"
  - "Your close associations with people should be with the achievers—never with the goof-offs, drinkers, drug users, lazy people, etc. Avoid those people as your associates, but always be pleasant to them, even if you don't approve of their lifestyle."

> **A key thing to remember throughout your life is to *stick with the winners.***

- **Take care of your body and mind.**
  - "Always work hard to control your temper, even in the worst of situations."
  - "Always be truthful and strive to be strong in character and body. A tired mind and body can't achieve—nor can a sick mind and body. Good rest, good sleep habits and good diet are essential."

- **Hard work beats talent.**
  - "You may know a person who does well academically in spite of the fact that he stays up late, drinks, etc. The fact is that he could do much better if he didn't."
  - "These are the people who have more native intelligence than others and who get by with a minimum amount of work—they are the losers, because in spite of their native intelligence, they are working against themselves

by doing the minimum necessary. They are developing a very bad habit that will follow them through life—*laziness*."

- "People with lesser native intelligence who are ambitious and reach their goals through hard work are the winners. These are the people employers want. I found that to be very true in law school. Those blessed with outstanding native legal ability never really made it in the practice of law—the hard workers did."

- **Read Shakespeare with a vengeance.**
    - "Some good lessons can be taken from great poets of the past—Shakespeare in particular. If you study Shakespeare in college, do it with a vengeance."
    - "I recall a Shakespearian soliloquy in his play *Hamlet* in which a father (Polonius) in seeing his son (Laertes) off, offered him advice based on Polonius's mature experiences—a father's attempt to mold good character in his son. As his son was leaving Polonius said:

- **Don't speak or act without careful thought.**
    - "Give thy thoughts no tongue [don't run off at the mouth or speak without thinking], nor any unproportioned thought his act [don't act without careful thought]."
    - "Be thou familiar, but by no means vulgar [be friendly, but not overbearing or rude]."

- **Cherish your true friendships.**
    - "The friends thou hast, and their adoption tried, grapple them to thy soul with hoops of steel [cherish your true friendships and hold onto them]. But do not dull thy

palm with entertainment of each new hatched, unfledged comrade [don't dirty your hands or waste your time being overly friendly and generous with every person you meet; even if they appear to be friends, don't accept them as true friends until their friendship is tried and established]."

- **When you have to fight, be brave.**
  - "Beware of entrance into a quarrel [avoid fights and arguments], but being in, bear'd that the opposed may beware of thee [if you can't avoid a fight or quarrel, then stand strong and don't be fearful]."

- **Be careful with your words.**
  - "Give each man thine ear, but few thy voice [listen to everyone, but speak your mind only when it has meaning and importance]."
  - "Take each man's censure, but reserve thy judgment [if someone is critical of you, just listen and don't form a quick judgment; give it consideration]."

- **Be frugal with money.**
  - "Neither a borrower nor a lender be [avoid borrowing or lending money] for loan oft loses both itself and friend [if you lend money you will often lose it and the friction will cause the loss of a friend] and borrowing dulls the edge of husbandry [the habit of borrowing will make you less frugal, less thrifty and adversely affect your ability to manage money]."

- **Be truthful to yourself.**
  - "This above all, to thine own self be true and it must follow, as the night [follows] the day, thou cannot then be false to any man [if you are truthful to yourself, it follows necessarily that you will be truthful with everyone—you will not be a phony]."
  - "Aside from Shakespeare, I often think of the lines written by Thomas Gray, who, while strolling through an ancient church yard (cemetery) wrote *Elegy Written in a Country Churchyard*. Thomas Gray looked at the old tombstones and thought of the people buried there—and he wrote:
  - "Full many a gem of purest ray serene, the dark unfathomed caves of ocean bear [he thought of the graves as dark, bottomless caves at the bottom of the ocean, many of which may contain beautiful gems, diamonds, etc.]."
  - "Full many a flower is born to blush unseen and waste its sweetness on the desert air [he thought to himself that many beautiful flowers—like the bodies buried there—are born and die—never to be noticed and never to have had a chance to show the world their sweetness and ability]."

- **Show the World Your Abilities**
  - What Thomas Gray was saying was that those people buried there may have been real gems—people of beauty and ability—who were born and died without ever having the opportunity to show the world their abilities.

- **Dad's Final Words**
    - "If nothing else, you have the chance to do and to be whatever you will, and as long as your mother and I are alive, we will always be there to help."
    - "But you can never count on us being there—not even for tomorrow. You must be prepared to stand on your own feet, and to make your success in life without anyone's help. You must start now."

CHAPTER 8:

HABITS FOR A HAPPY LIFE

How to Find Happiness, September 7, 2016

Dear Tim, Alek, and Lily:

    I am writing to you for two reasons: the written word is easier to digest and remember than the verbal, and I want to share with you a few of the mistakes and lessons I've learned. Take them for what they're worth.

TREAT YOUR BODY LIKE A TEMPLE

Being fat sucks. Make tough decisions, and get 100 percent compliant with your diet.

    Bad food is any food that is processed (e.g., hamburger, hot dog, bratwurst). Avoid processed food. Limit your intake of those foods from your diet, and eat real food (e.g., fruit and vegetables). Artificial food is bad; natural food is good.

If you had a million-dollar racehorse, would you let him eat at McDonald's? No way! Isn't your health more important than a horse? Treat your body like a temple.

DENY YOURSELF ONCE A DAY

Deny yourself of a guilty pleasure at least once a day. *Mind over body.*

Tempted by ice cream? Just say no.

FASTING

Don't eat anything or drink sugar water for eighteen consecutive hours. Mind over body—take control of your body.

EXERCISE ONCE A DAY

Do one exercise every day, no matter how small (e.g., twenty-five push-ups, one minute of planking/boat pose, or a one-to-two-mile walk or jog).

DRINK FOUR WATERS A DAY

Drink four sixteen-ounce waters a day. Water purifies the body.

WASH YOUR HANDS BEFORE MEALS

Wash your hands before meals, and you will rarely get sick.

WASH AND MOISTURIZE YOUR FACE

Wash and moisturize your face at the end of every day. This is the best way to keep a youthful appearance. When you get old, you'll be glad you did.

NO CAFFEINE

Avoid caffeine (e.g., coffee and soda). Artificially stimulating your heart is never a good thing.

Make Money Your Servant, Not Your Master

Big cars and fancy homes have never made anyone happy—they just make you want more stuff. You'll never win the race to keep up with the next guy down the block.

Material possessions will never make you happy, but travel will. Travel broadens horizons and brings new perspectives—it will make you more interesting, worldly, and fun.

SIMPLICITY

If you haven't worn a piece of clothing in thirty days, donate it to Goodwill. Get rid of the crap that clutters your space and mind.

WITHHOLD 14 PERCENT FROM EVERY PAYCHECK

Guaranteed path to financial wealth? Just withhold 14 percent from every paycheck, beginning with your first check. With the magic of automatic withdrawals, you will become an automatic millionaire.

Deposit two thousand dollars in a retirement account once a year for six years beginning at age eighteen. By age sixty-two, you will be a millionaire. Invest as early in your life as you can.

Live for the Moment

Live in the moment. Don't focus on tomorrow and what you'll be doing next week. Constantly focus on enjoying the very moment you're in, even if it's nothing more than your drive to work.

Don't live for some make-believe future that will never be as great as you think. The best moment is *right now*.

> **Don't live for some make-believe future that will never be as great as you think. The best moment is *right now*.**

HAPPINESS

Create a culture of service. Take your kids to the homeless shelter.

Mother Teresa was the happiest person in the world. Why? Mother Teresa dedicated her life to helping others.

> *The purpose of life is not to be happy. It is to be useful, to be honorable, to be compassionate, to have it make some difference that you have lived and lived well.*
> **—RALPH WALDO EMERSON**

GRATITUDE

Keep a gratitude journal. Once a day, write one thing in your journal that you are grateful for.

When you're feeling down, glance through your gratitude journal. You'll realize that things aren't as bad as they seem.

BEGIN WITH A POSITIVE FOCUS

Begin every family meal by sharing something in your life—personal or professional—that you are grateful for. Nothing bad can happen when you start from a mindset of gratitude.

Control Your Thoughts

The one thing you control is your mind. Watch out for negative thoughts.

When a negative thought enters your mind, make sure you're aware of it, and do your best to cast it out.

> *It is not what others do or even our own mistakes that hurt us the most; it is our response to those things.*
> **—STEPHEN R. COVEY**

DREAM BIG

Write down your top one hundred dreams in a journal.

Dream big, without limits. Dreams will never come true unless you believe in them. Share your dreams with your family and friends, and ask them to hold you accountable.

> *Just see how big you can blow up your life.*
> **—GARY KELLER,** *The One Thing*

BE PRESENT

Be in the moment when speaking with someone. Don't look away or think about anything except for one thing: the person speaking with you. Focus your entire attention on them.

BE HUMBLE

Never forget that you are no better than anyone else.

CHALLENGE EVERYTHING

Never accept what others tell you. Think for yourself.

BE YOURSELF

Life is too short to be normal. Who cares if people think you're different? Have fun and be yourself.

Spend Time in the Classroom of Silence

Spend ten minutes every day in the classroom of silence. Instead of saying a formal prayer, think silently about four things:

1. Gratitude: Something you are grateful for.

2. Best version of yourself: Something you did that helped you become a better version of yourself.

3. Forgiveness: Ask for forgiveness for the bad things you may have done.

4. Pray for others: Pray for someone in need.

Formal prayer is good, but it doesn't open your mind to thought and reflection. Spend time every day talking to God. Don't forget to ask, "God, what do you think I should do?" You will find answers to your questions in the classroom of silence.

Become a Lifelong Learner

Read books, and go to self-improvement seminars. Become a better version of yourself every day.

> *Work constantly to improve without becoming satisfied.*
> —JOHN WOODEN

TURN OFF THE TV

Live TV-free for thirty days, and watch your life change. Read a book, and spend time with your kids.

> *The challenge is not to manage time, but to manage ourselves.*
> —STEPHEN R. COVEY

STOP READING THE NEWSPAPER

Newspapers are full of negative crap that you can't change. Reading newspapers is a waste of time.

NO EMAIL IN THE MORNING

Do not read email before noon. Email is a distraction and distracts you from your priorities.

READ TEN PAGES OF A BOOK

Read at least ten pages of a book every day. Books change our lives.

*A man who doesn't read has no advantage
over a man who can't read.*

—MARK TWAIN

Nurture Relationships with Carefree Timelessness

The best way to nurture your relationships is carefree timelessness.

Block out the afternoon, and spend time with your kids, mother, high school buddy, or spouse. Go to a ball game with your kids. Carefree timelessness with your loved ones is priceless.

Kiss and Hug

Kiss and hug your spouse and kids every day, and tell them you love them. Never forget.

WRITE A LOVE LETTER

Write a love letter to your spouse, mother, or kids—tell them why you love them. They will treasure your letter and keep it forever.

STOP THINKING ABOUT YOURSELF

Always think of the other person's interests. Do not talk about yourself—find out as much as you can about the interests of the person you're speaking with.

Try to remember names, and refer to strangers by their first names. At public events go outside your comfort zone by meeting and getting to know a stranger.

Take a Dale Carnegie course on self-improvement.

THE SECRET TO A STRONG MARRIAGE

Do everything in your power to make your spouse happy. Don't keep score—just give as much as you can. If you care more about your spouse's happiness than your own, you will have an amazing marriage.

Always ask your spouse, "Is there anything I can do to help?"

> *If you place the other person's interests first, your interests will always be taken care of. Always.*
> **—BOB BURG**

Success Is in the Effort

Youth is wasted on the young who think they have an eternity to live. If you had twelve months to live, how would you live them? What's stopping you?

> *Live each moment with absolute certainty that you don't have a moment to spare.*
> **—JOHN WOODEN**

FIND YOUR PASSION

Work sucks if you're not happy doing it. Find your passion, and spend your life realizing it. If you are passionate about your work, it becomes fun.

EMBRACE YOUR FEAR

Put yourself through the fire of the most uncomfortable situations. Think of the things you've been holding off on, and do at least one a day. Make that call, shoot the video, or write that letter. It won't kill you, and you'll come out stronger every time.

LEAD BY EXAMPLE—NOT WORDS

Your kids will learn from your example, not from your words. Live a life of virtue, and your kids will follow your lead.

How do you live a life of virtue? By striving always to become the best version of yourself. That is the secret to life.

EFFORT COUNTS, NOT RESULTS

Strive always to give your best effort. If you give your best effort, the results are irrelevant. Only you know deep inside when you've given your best effort.

Success is giving 100 percent of your effort, body, mind and soul, to the struggle.

—JOHN WOODEN

No Substitute for Hard Work

There are no quick fixes. Success comes through hard work, lots of mistakes, and a willingness to die for your cause.

BE HUNGRY

Success is determined by one thing: raw, naked ambition. How bad do you want it? When you have a burning desire to accomplish something, the world will get out of your way to make it happen.

Create a Legacy

Do something that will help others after you're gone. Write a book, create a not-for-profit foundation, or make an impact through a charitable act of kindness. Leave your mark on the world.

> *It is, above all, to matter, to count, to stand for something, to have made some difference that you lived at all.*
> **—GARY KELLER,** *The One Thing*

CREATE A PERSONAL MISSION STATEMENT

Look far into the future. Think of where you want to be in twenty or thirty years, and write a vision plan for your life. If you can't dream it, it won't happen.

Write your Vision Plan in a book, and review it daily.

> *If you carefully consider what you want to be said of you in the funeral experience, you will find your definition of success.*
> **—STEPHEN R. COVEY**

STICK WITH THE WINNERS

Find the highest achievers, and stick with them.

> *You will become the average of the five people you spend the most time with.*
> **—JIM ROHN**

Take Action

Be a practitioner, not just a student. Take action, make mistakes, and then make more mistakes. This is where you'll find answers.

TAKE CHANCES

At the end of your life, you won't regret the things you did—you'll regret the things you didn't do. Take a chance. The worst that happens is you fail … and who cares?

> *Don't live in fear of making a mistake.*
> **—JOHN WOODEN**

NEVER TOO OLD OR YOUNG

Michelangelo worked on Saint Peter's Basilica until his death at age eighty-eight, Benjamin Franklin created bifocals at age seventy-eight, and John Keats wrote celebrated poetry before his death at the age of twenty-five. You are never too old or young.

INTERPERSONAL SKILLS

Try not to become a man of success, but a man of value. Look around at how people want to get more out of life than they put in. A man of value will give more than he receives.

—ALBERT EINSTEIN

CHAPTER 9:

HOW TO MAKE MAGICAL THINGS HAPPEN

My son thought I was crazy, and in hindsight, maybe he was right.

My then-eighteen-year-old son, Tim, and I were casually walking along Main Street in downtown Greenville, South Carolina, when Tim pointed out the gorgeous office building of Greenville's most prominent architectural firm. Tim mentioned words to the effect of "It would be incredible to work there someday," and I responded, "Let's go in and say hi."

Tim stopped dead in his tracks and looked at me with sheer terror. He responded, "Dad, you can't be serious. We can't just walk in there." I walked toward the front entrance, and Tim sheepishly followed. When we walked through the front door, we were greeted by a smiling and friendly receptionist who offered to introduce us to the managing partner of the firm, "Rip."

Rip showed us around the office and introduced us to many of the employees and then took us upstairs, where he spent one hour chatting with us in a private conference room overlooking the interior of the office. Tim and I could not have met a friendlier or more accommodating person. As we left that day, Rip provided his cell number and offered to stay in touch.

I did not waste that opportunity. Later that week, I called Rip, and we did more than stay in touch; we became good friends. Rip hosted our family on football weekends, treated us to meals in Greenville and Clemson, and most importantly has been a wonderful mentor and a trusted advisor for Tim during his college years at Clemson University. I treasure our friendship with Rip.

Was the encounter with Rip simply a chance encounter or pure luck? Some would say so, but I don't think so. That meeting with Rip was meant to be. In my view, God wanted Tim to have a mentor and a trusted advisor, and Rip Parks was the perfect person. And I could not be more grateful.

Of course, it would have been easy for Tim and me to just keep walking away from the front entrance of the prominent architectural firm. But walking through that front door led to an encounter—and ultimately a friendship—with one of the best men I've ever known. And just think: What is the worst that could have happened? Perhaps the receptionist would have told Tim and me to leave. We would have lost nothing.

Sometimes taking a chance is not risking anything. Instead, it's not taking the chance that is the real loss.

CHAPTER 10:

THE MOST POWERFUL SKILLS YOUR CHILDREN NEED

What skills have the greatest practical use for everyday life? Interpersonal skills. Yet interpersonal skills are not taught at universities, so you are left alone to figure this out for yourself.

But where do you begin? Dale Carnegie's classic 1936 book *How to Win Friends and Influence People* is the most powerful nonscriptural book ever written. Laden with simple and common sense principles, this book is a masterpiece on the subject of interpersonal relations. Almost tragically, most people have not read this book, and even fewer apply its principles.

When applied in the real world, the principles in *How to Win Friends and Influence People* will have a greater impact on your life than anything else. You will have a framework for meeting new people, engaging in their interests, and getting them to know, like, and trust you. Nothing is more powerful.

Eleven Proven Steps for Living a Life of Meaning and Influence

These are the principles that Dale Carnegie would want your children to know.

- **Step 1: How to begin a conversation.** *Never* talk about yourself. No one wants to hear you talk about yourself. Ask questions about the person's interests and passions (e.g., "What do you do for a living?"). And then find out as much as you can about their work and passions. People love talking about themselves, and they will appreciate your interest.

- **Step 2: Be present.** When you talk with someone, listen carefully to what they're saying. Make sustained eye contact. Don't look away, and do not think of anything other than what the person in front of you is saying. Let them know that you're listening and that you care what they say.

> *Most people do not listen with the intent to understand; they listen with the intent to reply.*
> **—STEPHEN R. COVEY**

As you learn new things from your acquaintance, respond to let them know that you heard what they said: "That's interesting. I never thought of that." Keep following up with questions until you've learned as much as you can about your new friend.

- **Step 3: Use first names.** Call everyone you meet by their first name. Everyone loves the sound of their name. Saying their first name repeatedly will help you remember their name.

> *A person's name is to that person the sweetest*
> *and most important sound in any language.*
> **—DALE CARNEGIE**

Frequently you will hear people confess, "I'm terrible with names." Everyone is bad with names, but there's a solution: repeat the first name of everyone you meet at least three times when you first speak with them. By repeating their name three times, you will reinforce their name in your memory. And the next time you meet them, your acquaintance will be surprised that you remembered their name.

- **Step 4: Talk with strangers.** Whenever you go to a social event, seek out at least one person you don't know and talk to them. Try to find out what makes the person tick (a.k.a. their passion for life).

> *Talk to someone about themselves,*
> *and they'll listen for hours.*
> **—DALE CARNEGIE**

Be bold and take the initiative. This might seem awkward at first, but you might find that you have more in common than you previously thought. And you might just make a new friend.

- **Step 5: Preparing to meet someone.** If you plan to meet someone (a new or existing relationship), find out as much about them as possible in advance.

If the person roots for the UConn women's basketball team, research the latest news about the UConn women's basketball team (even if you have no interest in them), and be prepared to discuss the team with your new friend (e.g., "Great win for the Huskies last night against their archrival"). It doesn't matter that you have no interest in UConn women's basketball; what matters is that your friend roots for them.

- **Step 6: Dealing with anxiety and stress.** Think of the worst possible outcome and accept it. Then work to create the best possible outcome. You will never be disappointed because you've already accepted the worst outcome.

> *Ask yourself: What is the worst that can happen? Then prepare to accept it. Then proceed to improve on the worst.*
> **—DALE CARNEGIE**

- **Step 7: Own your mistakes.** Do not blame others for your mistakes. When you screw up, own it (e.g., "I am sorry; this shouldn't have happened"). When you own your mistakes, others will be forgiving.

> *It raises one above the herd and gives one a feeling of nobility and exaltation to admit one's mistakes.*
> **—DALE CARNEGIE**

- **Step 8: Never disagree with someone in public.** Do not criticize, condemn, or complain.

> *There is only one way to get the best of an argument and that is to avoid it.*
> **—DALE CARNEGIE**

No one wants to hear that they're wrong (even if they are). Don't tell someone that they're wrong. Listen, nod attentively, and if necessary, tell them in private that you might not agree. Be kind and understanding.

- **Step 9: Do not hold grudges.** When you hold a grudge against another person, you are only hurting yourself. Forgive everyone, even those who hate you.

> When we hate our enemies, we are giving them power over us: power over our sleep, our appetites, our blood pressure, our health, and our happiness.
> **—DALE CARNEGIE**

- **Step 10: Your mindset.** No one cares about you (except your spouse—and they might not even really care). Everyone cares about themselves. Make every person you meet the center of the conversation, and get them to talk about themselves. Everyone—even those in prison—have something in their life that they are proud of (e.g., their children, hobbies, or work). Get them to talk about the things they love.

> **Everyone cares about themselves. Make every person you meet the center of the conversation, and get them to talk about themselves.**

> *You can make more friends in two months by becoming interested in other people than you can in two years by trying to get other people interested in you.*
> **—DALE CARNEGIE**

If you ask someone, "Would you mind sharing with me how you've become so successful?" you instantly make a new friend. Over the next twenty minutes, your new friend will tell you about their successes, and all you have to do is nod your head.

- **Step 11: Do not be transactional.** In most relationships, people think, "What can I get out of this?" Don't be transactional. Do not think about what someone can do for you. Rather, think of what you can do to help them.

> *The rare individual who unselfishly tries to serve others has an enormous advantage.*
> **—DALE CARNEGIE**

When you give without any expectation of getting anything in return, you will be rewarded tenfold. This is known as the rule of reciprocity. When you give something of value to others, they will want to return the favor.

The Greatest Power That You Have

The greatest thing you can do with your life will be to make a difference in the life of a less fortunate person. If you do this, you've lived a good life.

> *I believe we possess the greatest power in the universe, the power to make a difference in the life of another human being.*
> **—JON GORDON,** *The Carpenter*

CHAPTER 11:

THE SCARIEST DAY OF MY LIFE

June 2, 2010: One of the scariest days of my life.

On this day, I got the news that rocked me. During a routine day at my law firm, I was called into a meeting with the senior partners. The meeting began with small talk, and then one senior partner looked me squarely in the eyes and calmly said, "John, it's time we part ways."

This would be the beginning of the end of my dream job. On this day, I was shown the door after almost fourteen years of working at the only job I ever wanted. With a wife and three little children at home depending on me, I had no idea what I was going to do. For the first time in my professional life, I was scared.

Suddenly I was at a crossroads in my career. I did the only thing I could think of doing: I met with my clients to convey my gratitude for their trust and asked whether they would join me at my new law firm. One by one, I got an answer that I didn't take for granted: "Of course we will come with you. We wouldn't consider anything else." This was the beginning of my new professional life.

My Lifetime of Failure

I have to confess that I've failed miserably many times throughout my life.

- I was fired at my first job as a lawyer after only three weeks and two days on the job. The senior partner told me, "This isn't your bailiwick." (I agreed with him).

- My former partners laughed when I told them about my plan to write a book (*The Power of a System*) about law firm marketing and management. They questioned why I would give away all of the secrets (because no one else did).

- When my new law firm opened, I was on the losing end of three consecutive defense verdicts (including a loss of more than two hundred thousand dollars in case-related expenses).

- My new law firm lost seventy-two thousand dollars in our first year of operations.

- Friends laughed when I told them about my wife's plan to run a campaign for Supreme Court justice in New York (a member of her political party had not won a contested election in our judicial district in eighteen years).

Even when we think everything is going well, life surprises us with hardships and challenges that can seem insurmountable.

It seems that everyone puts on a facade of perfection. No matter how things are really going, you hear people say that "everything could not be better." Blah, blah, blah. Let's face it: everyone struggles. And even when we think everything is going well, life surprises us with hardships and challenges that can seem insurmountable.

Three Proven Tips for Overcoming Failure

My personal and professional life has been filled with one failure after the next. Each time I face failure, I question whether I am doing the right thing and sometimes question whether I should keep going. But even when I feel defeated and ready to give up, I try to keep moving forward.

TIP 1: NEVER GIVE UP

Thomas Edison, inventor of the light bulb, was once asked how many times he failed. Edison responded, "I have not failed ten thousand times—I've successfully found ten thousand ways that will not work." Edison had more than his share of failures, but no one heard about Edison's failures because he refused to dwell on them. Instead, Edison kept trying and never gave up.

> There are times we come up short. Times when the best efforts fail. Pouring our time, life, entire being into benefiting another human against odds which, ultimately, prove insurmountable leaves us depleted, drained, demoralized.
> If you have not stood in this isolated, dark, desolate place, you are not a trial lawyer.
> —**LEE PATTON, ESQ.**, St. Louis, Missouri

When you doubt yourself and want to give up, *never quit*. Success might be right around the corner.

TIP 2: LIVE IN DAY-TIGHT COMPARTMENTS

In Dale Carnegie's classic 1944 book *How to Stop Worrying and Start Living*, he teaches us to "live in day-tight compartments." This means living for today. Don't worry about what might happen tomorrow or down the road—only focus on the things that are within your control today.

> *It is not our goal to see what lies dimly in the distance but to do what clearly lies at hand.*
> **—THOMAS CARLISLE**

When I am in trial, I try not to worry about the outcome. Why? Because I don't control the outcome; a small group of six jurors decides who wins the trial. It isn't productive to worry about something that I don't control. I try not to worry about any aspect of the trial other than what I am doing that day.

TIP 3: FOCUS ON YOUR CIRCLE OF INFLUENCE

Try not to worry about things that you don't control. Stephen R. Covey, author of the classic book *The 7 Habits of Highly Effective People*, teaches us that there are two circles—namely, the *circle of concern* and the *circle of influence*. The circle of concern are those problems over which you have no influence (e.g., nuclear war, famine), while the circle of influence consists of a much smaller subset of the issues over which you control (e.g., your health, fitness, faith).

> *The place to begin building any relationship is inside ourselves, inside our circle of influence, our own character.*
> **—STEPHEN R. COVEY**

Why waste time watching the news and worrying about worldwide events over which you have no control? This is a waste of your time. Instead, focus on the things that you control (e.g., read five pages of a book, spend five minutes alone in prayer, learn meditation or yoga, or go for a jog). Don't worry about crazy dictators in foreign countries; instead, stop watching TV and get to work improving yourself, even in small ways.

Failure Can Lead to Surprising Results

Fast forward to a chance encounter with a defense lawyer in an elevator following a deposition. I had worked against this defense lawyer for more than fifteen years, and we knew each other well. Out of the blue, the defense lawyer bluntly said, "There's something I have to tell you. I've never seen you this happy." Perhaps for the first time, I realized that the scariest day of my life (ten years earlier) was also one of the best.

I have had more than my share of tough days, doubts, and defense verdicts. Life as a self-employed law firm owner is hard, and I never stopped second guessing myself, but the security and stability of a job was nothing more than playing it safe. While I had no idea at the time, I discovered over time that it is far more rewarding to work for my family. It just feels better.

Is it easy overcoming hardship, doubt, and struggle? Hell no. But no one ever said life was easy.

HEALTH AND NUTRITION

*Whether you think you can or think you cannot,
either way you're right.*

—HENRY FORD

CHAPTER 12:

HOW TO LIVE A LONG, HEALTHY LIFE

My father, James H. Fisher, Esq., was a workaholic. My dad went to work in the early morning hours, worked seven days a week and almost never took a vacation. My father was consumed by the love of the law, and our family was the lucky beneficiary. But there was a price to pay.

My father died at the age of seventy after years of surgery for cancer and peripheral vascular disease and diabetes. The final ten years of his life were very hard for my dad, but there is no one who loved life more. And I know my dad would love to be alive today more than anyone.

Just like my dad, you work your butt off to make a good life for your family. And your family is worth it—but not at the expense of your health. Let's face it: if you're overweight, don't work out, and are beginning to have health problems, you're not serving your family well. And you, too, will pay the price down the road.

These are the lessons I've learned about health and nutrition that I hope provide some value for you.

* * *

How My Best Friend Changed His Life

The awkward moment of silence with my best friend seemed to last forever.

As I was hanging out with my best friend and his wife in their living room, my best friend asked a simple question: "John, am I fat?"

Without wasting a second, I turned and looked at my friend in the face and responded matter-of-factly, "Yeah, you're fat." My best friend turned away from me, and he and his wife looked forward in total silence. We did not say another word.

AN OUTCOME THAT I NEVER EXPECTED

Six months later, I happened to have a chance encounter with my friend, and he asked, "John, do you notice anything different about me?"

I thought for a few moments, scratched my head, and responded, "No."

Then I got the shocking news: "I've lost seventy pounds."

Didn't see that one coming. And then my friend shared the story of his transformation.

When I told my friend that he was fat six months earlier, it was the first time anyone had been honest with him. Almost always, friends and family would tell my best friend that he was "big boned" or "a big guy who carried his weight well," but no one was willing to tell him the truth. Turns out, when I told my friend that he was fat, it was a wake-up call.

A LIFE-CHANGING TRANSFORMATION

My best friend and his wife joined Weight Watchers, and over that six-month period, he went from 313 to 240 pounds. My friend transformed his life. After losing the weight, my friend was no longer a diabetic and did not have to take any of the eleven medications he had previously taken. There's little doubt my friend added ten to twenty years to his life. It was a life-changing transformation for a great guy.

And my best friend deserves all the credit. My friend took control of his life, and the results were shocking. I had nothing to do with my friend's life-changing transformation other than one little thing: I told him the brutal truth.

The Best Thing You Can Do for Your Friends

You are not helping your friends by soft pedaling their problems. If you have a friend who has a health issue (e.g., obesity or an alcohol or drug problem), be straight with them. Your friend might not like the truth at first, but they'll know you're trying to help them. And it just might get them to make a change.

This is not easy, and your friend might not be receptive, but this is the best thing you can do. And it's the kind of thing that just might help change your best friend's life.

* * *

The Impact That Food Can Have on Your Life

Fad diets are full of miracle solutions for weight loss. The diets are not necessarily bad, but the promises are overhyped, and the solutions are never as easy as suggested. Let's face it: losing weight is hard.

Your health and fitness deserve better than fad diets.

Your health and fitness deserve better than fad diets. You deserve decades of empirical evidence reinforced by peer-reviewed medical journals to support your health and nutrition choices. Let's take away the guesswork. And there's no better place to begin than rural China.

What We Can All Learn from Rural China

Diseases in the United States and Europe ("diseases of the West"), such as cancer, diabetes, and hypertension, are virtually nonexistent in rural China. But there's more to this: health problems such as obesity, coronary artery disease, autoimmune diseases, and dementia are so rare in rural China that they are practically unheard of. So what is the secret of the Chinese?

You might think the Chinese have superpowered DNA, but they don't. When Chinese move to the United States or Europe, their rates of diabetes, hypertension, obesity, and cancer are just as high as our rates. Turns out, genetics is not much of a factor at all.

> Because these diseases of affluence are so tightly linked to eating habits, diseases of affluence might be better named "diseases of nutritional extravagance." **The vast majority of people in the United States and other Western countries die from diseases of affluence.**
> —**T. COLIN CAMPBELL, PHD,** The China Study

The secret of the rural Chinese? It's simple: the Chinese do not eat animals. The diet of the rural Chinese consists almost entirely of plant-based whole foods, such as vegetables, fruits, and whole grains. Dairy and animal-based products are simply not part of the diet of those in rural China.

The difference between rural Chinese diets and "Western" diets is enormous. The diet of affluent countries, such as the United States, is based primarily on the consumption of animal foods and dairy. On average, Americans consume 35 to 40 percent of our total calories as fat. The list of our fatty foods includes butter, cheeseburgers, French fries, milk, ham, and hot dogs. What is common about these foods? They are animal-based foods.

Many diseases of the affluent were rare until the last 120 years. But with a change in diet to animal-based products and dairy, Americans have high rates of coronary artery disease, heart failure, stroke, cancer, diabetes, and … well, you get the picture.

Statistics That Will Shock You

Still not a believer? Let's take a look at the statistics.

- Chinese breast cancer rates are only one-fifth those of Western women.
- American men die from heart disease at a rate almost eleven times higher than in China.
- Africa, Asia, and most of Central and South America have very low rates of colorectal cancer.
- The bone fracture rate in rural China is only about one-fifth that of the United States.
- Rates of Alzheimer's are low in less-developed countries.

The evidence is overwhelming. The most powerful weapon we have against cancer, heart disease, and diabetes is the food we eat. The bottom line is that plant-based foods are good, and animal-based foods are bad.

The Failure of the American Health Care System

The number-one killer in America is heart disease, which is responsible for more than 700,000 deaths every year in our country. Cancer, the second leading cause of death, kills over 550,000 a year in the United States, and the third leading cause of death is "medical care," responsible for more than 225,000 deaths annually in the United States.

The biggest risk factor or cause of coronary heart disease is high blood cholesterol. What is the biggest cause of high blood cholesterol? Animal-based fats. If you reduce your blood cholesterol level to less than 150, your chance of dying from heart disease is virtually eliminated. The solution? Stop eating animals.

> *The evidence we have now is already striking. A plant-based diet prevents a broad range of diseases.*
>
> **—T. COLIN CAMPBELL, PHD,** The China Study

There is little doubt that the American health care system has failed us. Our system of health care is focused entirely on the treatment of diseases rather than on their prevention. This is a horribly misguided approach. If our medical schools and physicians spent more time on preventative medicine, we would all be much better served.

Only Real Men Have Heart Disease

Some may discourage you from eating a plant-based diet. It's not manly to eat plants—real men eat bratwurst, filet mignon, and hamburgers.

Your friends and family will tell you that those who eat a plant-based diet "deprive" themselves of the pleasures of meat, but they also "deprive" themselves of the ravages of diabetes, cancer, hypertension, and coronary artery disease. Is that a trade off worth taking? You can be the judge.

* * *

What I Learned from a Farmer

This was an eye-opener, to say the least.

As I walk on a dirt path at his farm, I ask my friend Arnold—a farmer in his late fifties—whether he enjoys raising roughly sixty Angus cows, each weighing fourteen hundred pounds. The Angus cows follow Arnold wherever he walks in the hope of getting something to eat. Arnold replies quickly that, of course, he loves what he does, but there are drawbacks.

Arnold explains that the Angus cows have families, and in these families, the mother is inseparable from her calves. Once the calves reach nine months of age, the mother and her calves are physically separated, and they cry inconsolably for the next seventy-two hours. Arnold knows that every time this happens, he won't sleep for three days, and there's nothing he can do about it.

And that's not all. The cows know when they are about to be slaughtered, and they cry inconsolably about their imminent fate. Turns out that cows have many of the same emotions and feelings as humans.

Why I Stopped Eating Meat

I said nothing in response to Arnold, but I'd had no idea about what he told me. I just thought cows were a meal. It never dawned on me that cows were much more than merely living beings—they have feelings, emotions, and even families. How could I put these animals to death just so I could have a meal? It didn't seem right then, and it still doesn't.

On that day in October 2013, I stopped eating meat (although I eat fish on occasion), and I haven't missed a thing. I don't long for meat, nor do I miss it. I don't know if this has helped my physical health, but it just makes me feel better. And that's more than enough.

On December 16, 2016, Arnold died after living a life of humility and dedication to his family. I will always treasure my time with him, and it's about this time every year that I think of Arnold and how much I enjoyed spending time with him. God bless you, Arnold Elliott. You will be forever missed.

CHAPTER 13:

AN (ALMOST) GUARANTEED WAY TO LOSE WEIGHT

About a year ago, I met a friend whom I hadn't seen in about a year. As soon as I saw him, it was obvious my friend had lost a lot of weight. My forty-year old friend had gone from 270 pounds to about 205 pounds in less than a year, and the results were stunning. My friend went from appearing borderline obese (to be kind) to pretty close to slim and fit.

Trying not to be too intrusive, I eventually asked how my friend lost the weight, and his story revealed a secret to health and fitness that I will never forget. Of all places, it began at a mastermind meeting in Florida. My friend stated that he had a goal to lose a lot of weight but had struggled for most of his life with obesity and had tried every gimmicky diet program with little success. Then one of our mastermind members offered a unique solution.

The solution was simple. The two men promised to call each other every night at a specific time and discuss the effort that each had made that day to limit their food intake and eat healthy meals. On a scale of 1 to 10, each would do a self-assessment of their effort for that day, and they would track and share the results with others. Simple enough.

The Power of Daily Personal Accountability

Following the mastermind meeting, I had no idea if there had been any follow through, and I gave the conversation no thought until a year later, when I saw for myself the incredible results. Through the power of daily personal accountability, there had been a dramatic change in the course of a relatively young man's health and fitness. There's little question that years were added to my friend's life.

> **Eating healthy is not a choice that is made weekly or even daily—it's a choice that is made at every moment of the day, choice by choice.**

Here's the secret that was revealed: eating healthy is not a choice that is made weekly or even daily—it's a choice that is made at every moment of the day, choice by choice. It's great to have an accountability partner who will hold you accountable for the decisions you make, but the accountability must be daily. Otherwise, you will be tempted to take shortcuts with no repercussions.

If you have to report your success, or lack thereof, every day, you will be held accountable, and there will be no room to hide. Personal daily accountability is the secret to sustained weight loss.

A Solution That Will Work for You If You Want to Lose Weight

A personal daily accountability program exists that can work for you—it's called My Body Tutor (www.MyBodyTutor.com). Here's how My Body Tutor works: you are assigned a tutor (a.k.a. your accountability partner), typically a personal trainer with experience in nutrition. On the website of My Body Tutor, you will track your food consumption, exercise, sleep, and water intake and set goals for weight loss.

The daily personal accountability is what makes My Body Tutor special. At the end of each day, you report everything you've done that day—good or bad—on www.MyBodyTutor.com. The following morning, your tutor will evaluate the previous day's report and call you to provide a critique of your food intake and the nutritional content of your food. Your tutor will monitor your sugar and sodium intake and give you a push when you need to exercise more and eat in moderation.

The website for My Body Tutor provides customized graphs that show your progress in weight loss, frequency of exercise, sleep patterns, water intake, and more. Your tutor will encourage, inspire, and hold you accountable. There's nothing like it.

Make Health Your Number-One Priority

What's more important than your health? If you're not taking care of your health, you're useless to your family, your spouse, and your kids. But let's face it: weight loss is damn hard. We're all tempted to indulge at times, and it's hard to lose weight on a sustained basis without help.

Make a choice today to put your health first, and taking a look at My Body Tutor is a great place to start. And if you do, maybe a year from now, your friends will hardly recognize you.

* * *

Twelve Steps for Better Health and Nutrition

We all lack self-discipline. Sustained weight loss and self-discipline are hard for all of us. You are not alone in this struggle for better health.

During the last year, I placed an emphasis on the most important thing in life: health. I had more than my share of mistakes and indulgences, but over the course of twelve months, my body weight dropped from 193.6 lbs. to 165.6 lbs. Truth be told, I didn't think this was possible; I just thought I'm getting older, and excess weight was something that I had to live with. But that's not true.

This is what I've learned over the past year.

- **Step 1: Read nutrition labels.** Nutrition labels are a gold mine of information. What you believe is healthy food might not be. You might think that soup is healthy and nutritious, but soup is loaded with sodium. Prepackaged, processed foods are almost always very high in sodium, which will raise your blood pressure and retain water in your body. Stay away from processed foods whenever possible.

- **Step 2: Salads are God's gift.** Want to eat in greater moderation? Make a salad a part of lunch and dinner. When you eat a salad first at every meal (except breakfast), you won't be tempted to go back for a second or third serving of the main dish. Eating a healthy, nutritious salad is also a great way to clear out your digestive tract.

- **Step 3: Limit the indulgences to one.** When you go out to dinner, just have one indulgence. If you want to have a beer, then you will not have other indulgences (e.g., chips and salsa or bread).

- **Step 4: Avoid cereal.** Cereal is loaded with sugar (it has almost the same sugar levels as candy). Substitute oatmeal in place of cereal. Add mixed berries (blueberries, blackberries, strawberries) and nondairy creamer, and oatmeal can become a delicious and healthy choice.

- **Step 5: How to deal with temptations.** When you are tempted to have a treat, (e.g., a chocolate chip cookie), *pause* and wait a couple of minutes, and see if the temptation passes. You might ask, "Do I really need this indulgence?" After you pause for a minute or two, you might realize that you're OK without it.

- **Step 6: Never get hungry.** Never head into a meal hungry. Plan snacks for late morning (11:00 a.m.) and late afternoon (4:00 p.m.), so you're not starving at mealtime. A protein shake is a delicious and healthy choice for a snack (MRM Veggie Elite is a delicious and healthy choice). Raw nuts and No Cow protein bars are healthy snacks for the middle of a workday.

- **Step 7: Limit your consumption of simple carbs.** Whenever possible, eat wheat or multigrain bread. White bread contains highly processed flour and additives that make it unhealthy.

When you eat pasta or rice, choose wheat pasta and brown rice. Moderation is the key (one serving).

- **Step 8: Have an emergency plan.** When you've had a long day at work and you're tempted to eat anything when you get home, have an emergency plan in place. Specifically, what will you do when you're hungry and you don't have any plans for a meal? This is where we can get into trouble and will be tempted to snack on garbage food (potato chips). I have Beyond Beef burgers ready for emergencies. Vegan burgers are high in protein and taste great.

- **Step 9: Make a plan for travel days and special events.** When you have a vacation or travel plans, make a plan. Airports and sports arenas have virtually no healthy options, so you have to plan in advance and bring your own food. Most sports venues will allow you to bring food, so you can cook a healthy option (vegan burger) and bring it to the game. Then you can enjoy the game guilt free!

- **Step 10: Become an expert in nutrition.** Read *The China Study*, by T. Colin Campbell, PhD. *The China Study* is the most comprehensive book ever written about nutrition, and it will change the way you think about nutrition forever. Food is medicine. What you eat will either help or hurt you. Treat your body like you will live forever and your body will reward you.

- **Step 11: Track what you eat.** Track everything you eat. This only takes two minutes per day. When you track what you eat, you become more conscious of your decisions—good and bad—and you will become more deliberate and mindful. There is no need to track points (although that works for those in Weight Watchers). Make things easy and simple. Otherwise, you won't carry through.

- **Step 12: Consistency is the goal.** Slow and steady weight loss is the goal. If you lose too much weight too fast, it will not be sustainable. Do not starve yourself. This is not sustainable weight loss. Eat normal, healthy meals and aim for a half pound of weight loss per week. The progress will be slow, and you won't notice much of a difference at first, but over four to six months, you will see a difference, and in eight to twelve months, your world will change.

MENTAL HEALTH

The greatest gift you have to give is that of your own self-transformation.

—LAO-TZU

CHAPTER 14:

THE JOURNEY OF SELF-EXPLORATION

It was a recurring conversation and deep down, I was worried.

My daily conversations with my nutrition and fitness coach (at *MyBodyTutor*) usually sounded like a broken record. "I feel great", I told my tutor, "I have no aches or pains, I reached my ideal body weight and I have a lot of energy." But truth be told, I needed help.

I told my tutor, "I'm struggling with mental health. I have racing thoughts and I struggle with anxiety and stress. Sometimes I wake up in the middle of the night and my mind is full of worry about … EVERYTHING. I almost never sleep well. I could use help."

This is when my body tutor introduced me to meditation. Admittedly, I didn't do much at first and I had a healthy dose of skepticism, but with no other alternative, I was ready for a change and I began learning about meditation. Here's what I discovered.

The Benefits of Transcendental Meditation

Studies showing the benefits of transcendental meditation are abundant. Many highly successful businesspersons, athletes, and celebrities attribute their success to transcendental meditation. Ray Dalio (hedge fund owner), Jerry Seinfeld, Michael Jordan, and Paul McCartney (and the other Beatles) attribute their success in business, comedy, sports, and music to transcendental meditation. The radio celebrity, Howard Stern, kicked a 3½ pack per day cigarette habit within 1 month of starting to meditate.

Over 400 peer reviewed studies have shown wide-ranging benefits of transcendental meditation, including reduced high blood pressure, diminished stress and anxiety, better sleep and improved self-control, awareness and mood control, and higher cognitive functioning and creativity. The American Heart Association approved transcendental meditation as a complementary treatment for high blood pressure.

> *These gifts include better physical well-being and mental functioning. The joys and rewards of being in the zone and accelerated internal growth.*
> **NORMAN ROSENTHAL,** Super Mind

Those who experience transcendental meditation for the first time report major changes in their lives.

- "The effect on my sleep has been profound."
- "Meditation has sharpened both my senses and my awareness of the world around me."
- "I experience a wonderful, restful feeling."

- "The heightened experience stayed with me longer after the experience."

The empirically based evidence for transcendental meditation is overwhelming. Our society treats mental illness and physical disease with an abundance of high-priced medications, but, I thought, perhaps there is a simpler and healthier solution.

Perhaps a crazy thought, but what if we could eliminate many of the conventional remedies for anxiety and stress and replace them with a technique that offers calmness of mind, less stress, and greater creativity? This just might be worth a shot.

A Quick Overview of Transcendental Meditation

Transcendental meditation is not a philosophy or a religion and does not require a change in your lifestyle or diet. There is nothing to believe in. You can be skeptical and the technique works just as well. It does not focus on breathing or chanting, just a resting state of mind. Transcendental meditation is relatively quick to learn and easy to master and it can be done anywhere.

Think of the surface of the ocean. The surface of the ocean can be rough and turbulent, but even in stormy weather, the depth of the ocean is calm and peaceful. Our mind is like the ocean. Our waking thoughts are like the surface of the ocean that can be choppy and constantly changing (all of the things you're thinking of), while a deeper level of consciousness is like the depth of the ocean that is calm and peaceful (where you have no thoughts, but yet you are awake). Transcendence is the level of the mind—much like the depth of the ocean—that is already calm.

> *Meditate, dive within, and expand your consciousness. In so doing, you will change, and the world around you will follow.*
> **NORMAN ROSENTHAL,** *Super Mind*

There are 3 well known levels of consciousness: the waking state, sleep and dreaming. But there is a 4th level of consciousness (transcendence) that transcends these levels, a state of calmness, silence and inner serenity. This 4th level of consciousness is a deeper level of consciousness that is untapped by most, yet has the potential to change our lives. Athletes refer to transcendence as "the zone" where they are locked in and focused.

The 20-Minute Mental Spa Moment

Transcendental meditation is easy to learn in just a few days. Transcendental meditation is taught by a certified instructor over the course of 4 90-minute sessions. It can be done anywhere and is a silent technique with your eyes closed. Once learned, you practice transcendental meditation on your own with some occasional refreshers from your instructor.

With transcendental meditation, you will be taught to meditate for 20 minutes twice a day—once in the morning when you wake and again in the later afternoon, ideally before dinner. Just like an important business appointment, you can schedule your 20-minute meditation into your workday. There is no concentration or control of mind required.

> *Both the quality of our consciousness and the way that it affects us are keys to a good life.*
> **NORMAN ROSENTHAL,** *Super Mind*

Your instructor will give you a mantra, a word that will give access to the calm level of the mind. You will think of your mantra as you meditate. You do not have to sit on a mat or have a specific body position. Be comfortable and as you meditate, your mind will be naturally drawn to more satisfying thoughts—places in your mind where you want to be. Sooner or later, your thoughts will be gone and you may experience stillness, quiet, and your breathing slows down and your muscles relax. Norman Rosenthal, author of *Super Mind*, refers to this as the "quiet bliss of transcendence".

The Fourth Level of Consciousness: Transcendence

During meditation, you are not trying to control your thoughts. You let your mind go naturally where it wants, to a place that is more satisfying. And over time, you reach the point of transcendence, which is the absence of thoughts. During transcendence, you reach a state of calmness and inner peace. It is the best moment of your day.

> *The key to growth is the introduction of higher levels of consciousness.*
> **LAO-TZU**

And what happens after you meditate? Your calmness carries through the next few hours and you become less reactionary, more reflective and calmer. You don't yell and scream when things don't go your way and you pause and think before reacting. And perhaps most importantly, your energy levels will be boosted by twice-aday meditation. The benefits of transcendental meditation accumulate as you practice it more.

Questions You Might Ask

Why do you need a certified transcendental instructor? You can try meditating without an instructor, but that's like trying to golf without a teacher. You'll struggle. An instructor will guide you through the process in 4 90-minute sessions. Transcendental meditation does not take long to learn.

What if you don't have time to meditate or you can't meditate for the full 20 minutes? Some meditation is better than none at all. You may want to use a meditation app that alerts you when you reach 20 minutes.

Why do you spend 20 minutes in meditation? Research shows that it takes 20 minutes to reach the inner calm and absence of thoughts that transcendence offers. Why do you meditate twice daily instead of once? Research shows that you will only receive half of the benefits of transcendental meditation if you meditate once a day.

Why do you need transcendental meditation if you already have a therapist? If you're struggling with depression or anxiety, therapy works. But therapy might be only once every 1 or 2 weeks and what do you do with the rest of the time? Transcendental meditation eases your mind and provides a boost of calmness and creativity twice a day. Transcendental meditation is a wonderful compliment to therapy.

How to Get Started on Your Journey of Self-Exploration

A great way to get started is to read Bob Roth's book, *Strength in Stillness*, an excellent primer about transcendental meditation. Want to take the next step by speaking with a certified transcendental meditation instructor? There are transcendental centers throughout the US.

Go to www.™.org or call 888-532-7686. You can get an introductory meeting with a ™ coach and learn more about this powerful technique.

Transcendental meditation gives access to the level of the mind that is largely untapped. The potential benefits—both physical and mental—are enormous. And once learned, you will have transcendental meditation for the rest of your life.

FINANCIAL MANAGEMENT

The best way to predict the future is to create it.
—**PETER DRUCKER**

CHAPTER 15:

HOW YOU CAN BECOME A MILLIONAIRE

No one gets rich fast. They get rich slowly and with patience. Getting rich just takes small steps and a little discipline. The sooner you start investing, the less you'll have to save to reach your goals.

> *When you try to get rich quickly, you stay poor forever.*
> **—DAVID BACH,** *The Automatic Millionaire*

Saving early in your life is the key. And always keep in mind: lots of people with high salaries have no savings or investments.

Step 1: Fund a Roth IRA

A Roth IRA is a type of individual retirement account (IRA) that provides tax-free growth and tax-free income in retirement. With a Roth IRA, you contribute money that's already been taxed. Then, when you withdraw the money in retirement, you do not pay taxes.

If you contribute to a Roth IRA, you can always withdraw the money you contribute (the principal) penalty free. With a Roth IRA, you pay taxes on the amounts you contribute but not on the earnings. Your Roth IRA earnings won't be taxed at all. If you do this, you're saving thousands in taxes every year.

> *Every young person should have a Roth IRA, even if you're also contributing to a 401(k).*
> **—RAMIT SETHI,** *I Will Teach You to Be Rich*

Scenario 1: Start saving at age nineteen, and contribute $2,000 to your retirement account every year until you are age twenty-seven. From age twenty-seven to sixty-five, you contribute nothing. Assuming a 10 percent rate of return, you would have earned $1.02 million by age sixty-five.

Total investment: **$16,000 (eight years)**
Total value: **$1,035,148**
Earnings beyond investment: **$1,019,148**

Scenario 2: From nineteen to twenty-six, you don't invest anything. You start investing at twenty-seven, and contribute $2,000 to your account every year until you turn sixty-five. Assuming a 10 percent rate of return, you would have $805,185, despite contributing for more than thirty years longer.

Total investment: **$76,000 (thirty-eight years)**
Total value: **$805,185**
Earnings beyond investment: **$729,185**

The math doesn't lie. By investing early in your Roth IRA between age nineteen and twenty-six, you can sit back and do nothing after age twenty-six, and you'll be way ahead of the game. Ideally, you continually invest the maximum contribution to your Roth IRA and let the miracle of compound interest go to work.

If you invest in a Roth IRA, when the money is accessed at retirement age, it will be 100 percent tax free. If a thirty-year-old saves $500 per month in a Roth IRA until they are seventy years old, at a rate of return of 12 percent, they will have almost $6 million.

Step 2: Contribute the Maximum to an Employer-Sponsored 401(k)

Like a savings account or IRA, a 401(k) is simply a retirement investment account, one that's offered by your employer. The money you contribute to your 401(k) each year, typically a percentage of each paycheck, lowers your taxable income.

With the power of compound interest, saving even relatively small amounts of money can generate substantial wealth over time. Over a forty-five-year period, investing $100 per month at an 8 percent return generates over $500,000 in wealth. At a 9 percent return, the amount jumps to almost $750,000.

Investing early is powerful due to compound interest, which is any interest earned that accrues interest on itself. The earlier you put money away, the more it will grow. In a study, 80 percent of millionaires said that investing in their employer-sponsored retirement plan was the main way that they reached millionaire status. Seventy-three percent mentioned the habit of saving money regularly.

Save at least 14 percent of your gross income. Most people pay everyone else before themselves, but you should pay yourself first from every dollar you make. You should arrange to have money automatically taken out of your paychecks and automatically deposited into your 401(k) account.

> How rich you are depends on the amount you're able to save.
> —**RAMIT SETHI,** *I Will Teach You to Be Rich*

With a 401(k), your money is sent into your investment account without you having to do anything. Connect your paycheck to your 401(k) so that it's automatically funded. Here's the beauty of automatic withdrawals from your paycheck:

- It doesn't require discipline.
- You won't have to have a budget.
- The system works while you sleep.

Does this work? Let's say you have $100,000 and put it into your 401(k). You let it grow at 10 percent a year and never add another dollar. In thirty years at 10 percent interest, you'd have $1,744,940. The money grows tax deferred.

Most Americans get to the age of sixty and have nothing to show for it. You have to avoid this mistake by saving early.

Step 3: Start Investing Early

Start early. Start now. It's never too late to start. It's tempting to think that you've got plenty of time to invest when you get older, but the most crucial time to begin is in your late teens and early twenties.

Start early. Start now. It's never too late to start.

The miracle of compound interest. Would you rather have $1,000, or would you want to double a penny every day for a month?

If you double a penny every day for thirty days, you'll have $0.01 on day one, $0.02 on day 2, and $0.04 on day 3, and so on. If you keep accruing 50 percent interest on your whole investment every day, you'll have $163.84 on day 15, and on day 20, you have $5,242.88. As you keep doubling the number, you'll end up with $5,368,709 at the end of thirty days.

Every dollar you invest today will be worth many more tomorrow.
—**RAMIT SETHI,** *I Will Teach You to Be Rich*

That's the miracle of compound interest. As you continue to earn interest on your initial investment as well as the interest that accrues, you'll grow your wealth more and more quickly. The cardinal rule of investing: Keep investing regularly by making a contribution from every paycheck to your 401(k) account.

Step 4: Be Frugal, Avoid Debt, and Save Money

Just because someone lives in a big house and drives a fancy car doesn't mean they are wealthy. Most people with big houses and expensive cars are living beyond their means and are not wealthy.

Energy, thrift, and diligence are how wealth is built, not dumb luck.
—**DAVE RAMSEY,** *The Total Money Makeover*

When in doubt about a purchase, don't. You can always buy later.

Avoid credit cards. Don't get suckered into credit card debt, and avoid offers for credit cards with introductory offers and low APRs. Credit card companies make a fortune from such offers.

> *Broke people use credit cards. Rich people don't.*
> **—DAVE RAMSEY,** *The Total Money Makeover*

If you need a credit card, use debit cards that are linked to a checking account.

Do not buy expensive stuff. Spend as little as possible on cars. Buy used cars and drive them for at least seven years. New cars have a huge depreciation in value during the first couple of years.

> *Being willing to delay pleasure for a greater result is a sign of maturity.*
> **—DAVE RAMSEY,** *The Total Money Makeover*

Learn to negotiate everything. The days of impulse buying are over. Whenever you can, buy everything in cash.

Create a monthly budget. First, you have to have a written plan. Create a new budget every month, and tell your money what to do. When you write down what you are going to do with money, you are telling your money what to do. Your income minus your expenses is your disposable income. You can always spend more than you make; live below your means.

> *A budget is just telling your money what to do, instead of wondering where it went.*
> **—DAVE RAMSEY,** *Dave Ramsey's Complete Guide to Money*

Ninety to ninety-five percent of American households operate without a detailed accurate outline of income and expenses. This gives them only a slight clue whether they can meet their financial obligations every month.

- How much is your monthly income?
- How much a month do you spend on food, electricity, phone, gas, clothes, car maintenance, cable or satellite TV, car and home insurance, entertainment and rent/mortgage payments?
- What are your debts? How much do you spend a month on credit card debt(s), student loans, and mortgage or rent?

List and itemize all of your fixed and variable household expenses. A written budget will only take two to three hours to create and only needs to be reviewed for fifteen minutes every week.

Get a money mentor. You should seek out the opinions and guidance of experts in money management. Have a money advisor to hold you accountable.

> *The man, woman, or couple who makes significant financial decisions without careful consideration of outside counsel is destined for pain and heartache.*
> **—DAVE RAMSEY,** *Financial Peace Revisited*

You need a money mentor who will hold you accountable and kick your butt when you want to buy the seventy-five-inch TV with no cash down.

Create an emergency fund. The goal is to have three to six months of gross income for the emergency fund. An emergency is an event that you cannot plan for (e.g., unexpected medical expenses), not an expected expense (e.g., college tuition). Keep the emergency fund in liquid form (e.g., a money market account).

First, you need to set the actual amount of the emergency fund.

- What is your gross income per month?

- Multiple your monthly gross income by three: $_____. This is the minimum amount you should have in an emergency fund.

- Multiple your monthly gross income by six: $_____. This is the maximum you should have in an emergency fund.

- The range you want as a goal for the emergency fund is $_____ (minimum amount) to $_____ (maximum amount).

Credit: Dave Ramsey, *The Total Money Makeover Workbook*

Become an expert in money management. Knowledge is power. The best money management book of all time is *I Will Teach You to Be Rich*, by Ramit Sethi. Read this book first.

> We buy things we don't need with money we don't have in order to impress people we don't like.
> **—DAVE RAMSEY,** The Total Money Makeover

Read all of Dave Ramsey's books, including the following:

- *The Total Money Makeover*
- *Dave Ramsey's Complete Guide to Money*
- *Financial Peace Revisited*

Step 5: The Best Investments

Long-term investing works. Buy stocks of excellent companies, and don't sell them. Do not buy stock in a company based upon its product. Products quickly become obsolete, but a well-run company can last a long time.

Buy stock in companies that treat their employees well. If the employees love the company that they work for, they will treat the customers well, and in return, the company's profit will grow (and the stock price will rise). Employee satisfaction is a formula for long-term success.

> **Long-term investing works. Buy stocks of excellent companies, and don't sell them.**

Fortune magazine's "Top 100 Companies to Work For" provides a list of the best companies to work for, and without fail, the same companies appear on this list every year.

> *Buy and hold investing wins over the long term, every time.*
> —**RAMIT SETHI,** *I Will Teach You to Be Rich*

My favorite companies are (in order of preference)

- Apple,
- Adobe,
- Google,
- Costco,
- Stryker, and
- Novo Nordisk.

What do these companies do well? They are continually ranked among the top one hundred companies to work for in the world. The stocks of these companies will steadily increase in value in time because their commitment to employee satisfaction is the best in the world.

Step 6: Invest in Your Personal Development

The best investment that you will ever make is in yourself. Invest in seminars and professional development and leadership programs (e.g., Strategic Coach) that will make you the best version of yourself.

> *If you invest in yourself, the potential return is limitless.*
> **—RAMIT SETHI,** *I Will Teach You to Be Rich*

Investing in your own self-development is a far better investment than stocks and bonds.

Step 7: The Benefits of Self-Employment

There is no such thing as a permanent job working for others. When you work for others, you work at your employer's whim and discretion, and you can be terminated at any time (fair or not). Being self-employed gives you much more control over your financial future.

> *Many millionaires told me that their financial success is a direct function of owning a specialized business in a geo-area that contains little or no competition.*
> **—THOMAS J. STANLEY, PhD,** *The Millionaire Mind*

When you are self-employed, you reap the rewards of your labor, and no one can tell you what to do. There is nothing more gratifying.

The Crossover Point

The ultimate goal is financial freedom, a.k.a. the "crossover point," at which your investments earn enough to fund your expenses. If you do this, you'll be set for life financially.

FAITH

We cannot serve the Lord if we do not have a heart of forgiveness.
—MONTY WILLIAMS

CHAPTER 16:

A STORY OF HOPE

At first, it seemed like just another day.

When I got home from work in the summer of 1997, I mindlessly began talking about my day at work, oblivious as to whether my wife was listening. But something was a little different with my wife, and I could just tell from the expression on her face that something was not right. Lisa just stood there and looked at me, and finally, when I stopped talking, she delivered the devastating news: my mother had been diagnosed with colon cancer.

Shocking News that Floored Me

My mother had been the picture of perfect health; she worked out, ate right, and always took care of herself. Now, for the first time in my life, I was faced with the brutal reality that no child could ever be ready for—the potential mortality of the person who brought you into this world.

I called my mother that night as she faced the real prospect of a life cut short by cancer—a life that had seemed destined for many more years was now at risk of being cut short. On the phone with my mother that night, I heard the fear in her voice as we cried together.

The medical plan was simple enough. A surgeon would operate to remove the tumor from my mother's colon, biopsy the surrounding tissue, and days later tell us whether the cancer had spread. Whether my mother would live or die would not be known for days. And that night in my brownstone apartment in downtown Albany, New York, would turn out to be one of the longest nights of my life.

My mind raced with bitter thoughts that night. How could this happen? Why would God take my mother from us when she had been so careful about taking care of herself? My (future) kids might not meet their grandmother.

The Most Difficult Night of My Life

I knew there was no way I could sleep that hot and humid summer night. Filled with fear and anxiety, I left my apartment to walk the streets of downtown Albany. I walked around looking for some consolation and comfort, but the streets offered nothing. The church was locked and closed up tight, and no friendly stranger crossed my path to offer a word or gesture of comfort. I was on my own that night.

When I got back to my apartment, I knew that sleep would be an exercise in futility. This would be a long night of tossing and turning and envisioning a future without my mother. My wife was asleep in our bedroom, and as exhausted as I was, I had to fend for myself on the couch in our living room. I sat on the beat-up plaid couch consumed with fear and anxiety as the night dragged minute by minute into the early morning hours.

In an Instant, Everything Changed

It was well after midnight when, for what seemed like no reason at all, I just happened to spot a book on the bookshelf in our living room. I got off the couch, grabbed the book off the shelf, and randomly opened the middle of the book. Right there on the first page I looked at, my eyes focused on these words:

> *Lord, make me an instrument of thy peace.*
> *Where there is doubt, faith.*
> *Where there is darkness, light.*
> *Where there is sadness, joy.*
> *O divine Master, grant that I may not so much seek*
> *To be consoled as to console,*
> *To be understood as to understand,*
> *For it is in giving that we receive, and*
> *It is in dying to self that we are born to eternal life.*

As I read these words, I could almost feel the fear and anxiety drain out of my face and leave my body. Almost magically, I knew at that moment that God had a plan for my mother, and whether that was life or death, who was I to question God's will? For the first time since I had gotten the frightening news earlier that evening, I was completely at ease.

Maybe it's a bit hard to believe, but I know now that the words of Saint Francis were meant for my eyes that night. A sleepless night turned into one of hope

> **I knew at that moment that God had a plan for my mother, and whether that was life or death, who was I to question God's will?**

with the knowledge that, good or bad, God's will would be done. And it was up to me to be the source of hope and comfort (and possibly consolation) for my mother, sisters, and father.

The Fateful Day Finally Arrives

Several days later, my mother had the surgery, and my mother, dad, sisters, and I met with the surgeon to learn my mother's fate. I could see the anxiety and fear etched into the faces of my sisters, father, and mother as we huddled together in a small room in the hospital, but while this would have seemed hard to believe days earlier, I was at ease and hopeful. I gave a few words of hope and optimism to my family members, knowing that God had a plan for my mother and we were just about to find out what that was.

When the surgeon finally gave us the fantastic news that the cancer had not spread, we all broke down into tears. It was a collective sigh of relief for my family members after days of stress and worry.

I knew that my mother would make it, and I would get the chance to share this beautiful person with my future children. But in the end, it wasn't this life or death news that relieved my anxiety-ridden mind ... it was a dusty old book sitting on a bookshelf that had words of hope, consolation, and comfort.

It's never too late to give thanks for the special gifts in our lives. Thank you, Saint Francis, for the courage and hope that your words gave me when I needed them the most.

CHAPTER 17:

THE MOST POWERFUL QUESTION YOU WILL EVER ASK

In the tiny, cramped doctor's office, my wife and I waited to get the news that would change our lives forever. Our fate rested in the hands of a doctor whom we barely knew.

The doctor walked into the room and told my wife and me, "I've got good news and bad news. The bad news is that you will never have a child by natural means. The good news is that we can give you a family with science [artificial conception]." That wasn't for me. I got up, thanked the doctor, and walked out.

Later that night, I sat alone in the classroom of silence with God and asked the most powerful question you can ever ask:

"God, what do you think I should do?"

When I ask this question, there's usually no answer. But deep within my conscience,

> I sat alone in the classroom of silence with God and asked the most powerful question you can ever ask: "God, what do you think I should do?"

God sometimes gives the answers to life's most difficult questions, and on this night, God spoke to me: "There are babies waiting for you." I knew what to do.

Our Adoption Story

I had always wanted to adopt, and this gave us the perfect opportunity. So my wife and I went to Russia to adopt two babies. Our adoption agent told us that we would know who our children would be as soon we saw them, and she was right.

At the orphanage, my wife and I were handed two tiny baby twins, Boris and Liliya. We instantly fell in love. The tiny twins were the most beautiful gift we could ever hope for, and we knew we had found our children. But then life threw a curveball at us.

An aide at the orphanage brought us another baby, Oleg. Again, Lisa and I fell in love from the moment we saw our "dancing baby" and knew that Oleg was our son. But we had a problem: we had come to Russia to adopt two children, and we had no plans for a third (and had no clue how to care for two babies, let alone three).

When I went to our apartment in Russia later that night, I kneeled down in the classroom of silence with God and asked the most powerful question you will ever ask:

"God, what do you think I should do?"

Deep within my conscience, God answered my question: "These babies are my gift for you." A difficult question provided a clear answer: my wife and I knew that Boris, Liliya, and Oleg were our children.

A Family of Two Becomes a Family of Five

Five months later, Lisa and I attended a court proceeding in Russia to finalize the adoption of Tim (Boris), Lily (Liliya), and Alek (Oleg). At the hearing, the judge asked why we had come to Russia. I told the judge that my wife and I wanted to have children who looked like us, but that was only a partial truth. The full truth is that God told us to come to Russia to receive the greatest gift he could ever give. Deep within my heart, I knew this was the truth.

Moments later, the judge granted our adoption, and a family of two became a family of five. None of this would have happened if we had not asked the most powerful question you will ever ask: "God, what do you think I should do?"

It's easy to ignore this story and think that God doesn't answer prayers. But I know that sometimes God does. You just have to ask God the most powerful question you will ever ask ... and if you do, you might get an answer that you never expected.

* * *

Do You Believe in Miracles?

A start-up law firm was facing its first major challenge ... and I had no idea what to do.

In our first few months of operating our firm, we faced our first cash crunch—our operating account was running low, and our reserves were tight. No one told me that running a law firm would be this hard. We were running out of options, and I had more than my share of stress and anxiety. But there was hope.

We had settled a substantial malpractice case in federal court against the United States, and once the settlement funds were received, our cash flow issues would be resolved. But there was a catch—the US attorney told me that the settlement funds might not be available for as long as six to twelve months. This did not help. My mind was spinning with anxiety.

One day, on my way to a court conference, I happened to arrive early and decided to take a few minutes to step into a nearby church in downtown Albany, New York. I knelt at a pew and spent a few minutes in silence with God. I put my concerns on the table and gave them to God.

In a few moments of silent prayer, I told God about my dilemma, and I had a humble request. If it were God's will—and only if it were God's will—I asked if there were anything he could do to help expedite the receipt of the settlement funds. I realized that was a self-serving request, but I needed help, and I decided to put my problem in the hands of God.

As I was opening the back door to leave the church, I turned on my cell phone, and almost simultaneously, I heard a ping alerting me to a text message that read, "The settlement funds have been received." OK, I realize God can work miracles, but even this was almost too hard to believe.

That day I was reminded that when we put our problems and fears in the hands of God and trust that God will do what is best for us, things tend to work out. Our struggles will bring out the best in us—we just need to trust that God is by our side the entire time.

CHAPTER 18:

AN OPEN LETTER TO MY FRIEND, AN ATHEIST

When it comes to living a good life, no one has the moral high ground. One of my closest friends is an atheist, and he is one of the best people I've ever known.

When I speak with my friend openly about faith, we quickly realize we have more in common than we think. I think it's important to share our common ground. This is my attempt to share some common ground with my friend, an atheist.

1. We All Have Doubts

Faith is not something that is capable of certainty. A person with faith believes in the absence of knowledge. That is the essence of faith—we choose to believe without certainty.

Jesus's apostles doubted him. According to the Greek scriptures, Jesus was resurrected from the dead and lived publicly among his apostles and many others for forty days. Even after spending time with the resurrected Jesus, his apostles doubted what they had seen, according to the scriptures (Matthew 28:16–20: "When they all saw him, they worshiped, *but they doubted*").

A person cannot have a strong faith unless they continually challenge the basic precepts of faith. Yes, doubting is a good thing. If you have doubts, that means you are challenging your faith, and as a result, your faith will become stronger, or you will lose it. But even after challenging your faith, you will still have doubts, and there's nothing wrong with that.

2. Study the Life That Jesus Lived

Regardless of who you believe Jesus was—the Messiah, an imposter, or a myth created by his followers—study his life, and learn as much as you can about the life that he lived. Can you find anything about Jesus's life that is not centered upon love, radical mercy, and extreme compassion for the sick, disabled, social outcasts, and imprisoned?

Unfortunately, many people, including many atheists, do not study the life of Jesus. Instead, most are too busy to research the life of Jesus. And that's unfortunate because studying and contemplating the meaning of life are the most important things we can do.

3. Consider the Odds

When you think about the existence of God, consider the odds. Atheists have no explanation for the existence of life, and most argue that they will "figure it out" with time. Some claim that rocks collided, and a rudimentary life form sprung from the collision. OK, but if you are basing your beliefs on science and logic, these explanations are very unscientific. And if two rocks collided to create life, who created the rocks?

British physicist Stephen Hawking postulated that the creation of the world was formed by millions of extremely unlikely contingencies and that the world would not exist if the contingencies had not all occurred within a fraction of a second. How likely is this? It is more likely that you would win the lottery with odds of ten million to one ... twice.

When you look into the beauty of the sky and the universe we live in, it's hard to believe that a higher being does not exist. If God does not exist, who made this incredible universe, the beauty of nature, the magnificent animals, and our intellect? The odds of this occurring in the absence of a higher being seem extraordinarily remote.

> **When you look into the beauty of the sky and the universe we live in, it's hard to believe that a higher being does not exist.**

4. Bad Things Happen in the Name of Religion

Without a doubt, history is rife with war, violence, and death that have been done in the name of many religions, including Christianity. Evil can never be justified.

But the real question is whether the acts of evil would be approved by Jesus. To the contrary, Jesus's fundamental teachings were based upon radical mercy, love, and forgiveness. Jesus did not condone violence or retribution of any kind.

5. The Existence of Evil

Why would God allow evil to exist? This is the most difficult question. A relationship with God is dependent on our freely made decisions—we can accept or reject the relationship.

Similarly, we can be altruistic and generous, or we can live a monastic life or harm others for no reason. God cannot force us to be good, because otherwise we would be deprived of our ability to choose good over evil. Evil exists because we are autonomous human beings who must make choices to accept or reject our relationship with God.

What about natural catastrophes, such as the tsunami in the Indian Ocean that killed nearly 230,000 in 2004? No one can explain that. I have to believe that is part of God's plan that I just can't understand. Is that a good explanation? Of course not—it's a matter of faith.

6. Keep an Open Mind

I would ask my friend to keep an open mind. Consider the arguments for and against the existence of God, and form an independent judgment that is based upon a thorough understanding of the literature and scriptures. And if my friend does this, I will respect his quest for the truth.

My best friend once said that he would believe if God stood in front of him. Truth is, I doubt that would be enough. It might be enough to frighten my friend into temporary belief, and perhaps he would hold onto his beliefs for some time, but ultimately he would likely doubt what he had seen, just like Jesus's apostles.

I would tell my friend that many believe that God did live on earth in the form of a refugee peasant who was mocked and ridiculed and gave his life as a sacrifice for the sins of many. If that is not enough of a sign of God's existence, what will suffice?

7. Read Isaiah 53

I would leave my friend by asking him to reflect upon the prophesy set forth in chapter 53 from the book of Isaiah that was written seven hundred years before Jesus's life:

> *He had no beauty or majesty to attract us to him, nothing in his appearance that we should desire him.*
>
> *He was despised and rejected by mankind, a man of suffering and familiar with pain.*
>
> *Like one from whom people hide their faces, he was despised, and we held him in low esteem.*
>
> *Surely he took up our pain and bore our suffering, yet we considered him punished by God, stricken by him and afflicted.*
>
> *But he was pierced for our transgressions, he was crushed for our iniquities; the punishment that brought us peace was on him, and we by his wounds we are healed.*
>
> *He was oppressed and afflicted, yet he did not open his mouth; he was led like a lamb to the slaughter and as a sheep before its shearers is silent, so he did not open his mouth.*
>
> *By oppression and judgment he was taken away. Yet who of his generation protested? For he was cut off from the land of the living, for the transgression of my people he was punished.*

He was assigned a grave with the wicked, and with the rich in his death, though he had done no violence, nor was any deceit in his mouth.

Yet it was the Lord's will to crush him and cause him to suffer and though the Lord makes an offering for sin, he will see his offspring and prolong his days, and the will of the Lord will prosper in his hand.

After he has suffered, he will see the light of life and be satisfied; by his knowledge my righteous servant will justify man, and he will bear their iniquities.

Therefore I will give him a portion among the great, and he will divide the spoils with the strong, because he poured out his life unto death, and he was numbered with the transgressors.

For he bore the sin of many, and made intercession for the transgressors.

* * *

What God Wants Most

Before leaving for a trip to Israel, I was told by others that the trip would be transformative for my faith. Not knowing what to expect, I was a bit skeptical. Just as with any vacation, my wife and I planned to visit the popular tourist destinations, and I thought our friends' comments were likely nothing more than hyperbole. I had no idea what to expect.

Our first day in Israel was spent in Calvary in Jerusalem (the site of Jesus's crucifixion). We woke at 4:00 a.m. and arrived at 5:00 a.m.

As we walked into the Church of the Holy Sepulchre (on the site of Jesus's crucifixion), we viewed the anointing stone, where Jesus's body was anointed following his crucifixion. My mind and spirit have never been captured more by any other experience—words cannot describe what I felt in that moment.

Tears streamed down the face of those making the pilgrimage as they kneeled in deep prayer at the anointing stone. I will never forget this moment. And as I left the Church of the Holy Sepulchre, I wanted nothing more than to return.

Every day of our pilgrimage seemed to be better. We visited Jesus's birthplace in Bethlehem (six miles from Jerusalem), the Mount of Olives, the Garden of Gethsemane, as well as Nazareth, Jericho, and the Sea of Galilee in Northern Israel. By the end of our trip, we had formed friendships with priests, seminarians, brothers, a former nun, orthodox Jews, Muslims in the West Bank, and people just like us, who talked openly about their spiritual journeys.

The real value of a pilgrimage is that you get to explore your faith and belief in God. You face your doubts and questions and spend time with God in prayer while others on this spiritual journey lend their support and talk candidly about their faith experiences. You come to realize that you are not alone in the questions and doubts in your mind, and by confronting these questions, your faith grows stronger.

It is the time that we spend in quiet reflection and prayer that deepens our relationship with God. This is the one thing that God wants more than anything else: our time. And spending seven days in Israel provided a spiritual journey that was unlike any trip I have ever taken.

CHAPTER 19:

WHAT WOULD JESUS DO?

During a dinner I was having with two Jewish friends, one happens to casually mention to the other, "What if we're wrong [about Jesus]?" There was no response; it was a quiet and slightly awkward moment for a few seconds. I should have spoken up, but I held my tongue. This is what I wanted to say.

First, let's throw away the labels of who Jesus was. Instead, let's focus on the life that Jesus lived. When you study Jesus's life, there's only one conclusion: Jesus was a radical. Radically different, yes, but that alone would not be completely accurate. If only two words could be chosen to describe Jesus's life, they would be *radical mercy*.

If only two words could be chosen to describe Jesus's life, they would be *radical mercy*.

Jesus did not come to judge others. Rather, Jesus lived to take care of the poor, disabled, and weak, and his compassion and love focused on those who needed it the most—namely, criminals, tax collectors, and prostitutes—the outcasts whom society despised. Jesus knew that material possessions meant nothing, and instead, he lived a life devoted to serving those most in need.

Jesus returned violence and hatred with love, compassion, and mercy. Jesus's mercy was so radical and bizarre that it seemed unhuman. Even in the final moments of his life, Jesus displayed radical mercy. Among the final words out of Jesus's mouth were, "Forgive them, Father. They know not what they do."

If you study Jesus's life and try to emulate his lifestyle, you would live a life of unimaginable riches. For those who have attempted to live Christlike lives, their lives have focused on service to the poor, sick, and disabled.

History is full of examples of those who attempted to emulate Jesus's life of service and compassion. Mother Teresa took care of the poorest of the poor in Calcutta, India—not to convert them to Christianity but because she was emulating the life of Jesus.

Just for a moment, let's throw away the labels (e.g., Messiah, prophet, fraud), and try to imagine how Jesus would live if he were by our side right now. Why? Because if we disregard the labels, we can focus on a way of life that can transform our lives. And that, in my view, is a special gift for all of us.

This is how I believe Jesus would live today.

The Disabled

Jesus would celebrate the uniqueness of the disabled. No one gets to determine the worth of those with disabilities—that comes from God alone. When asked why a man was blind since birth, Jesus responded that it is "so the works of God can be seen" (reading from John).

All people are children of God. People with mental disabilities, such as Down syndrome and cerebral palsy, are compassionate and loving, and their hearts are as full as they come. The disabled have unique gifts that others don't have. For outsiders, it is hard to comprehend the problems faced by the disabled, and as a result, they are often misunderstood.

You are exactly what God had in mind when he made you.
—FATHER GREGORY BOYLE

Our worth is not determined by what others say about us. Similar to the disabled, Jesus's worth was not determined by the opinions of others. Our worth comes from God.

The Poor

Jesus was from a refugee family. Jesus told his disciples, "I will not leave you as orphans" (John 14:18). Jesus goes to be with the poor—he doesn't send someone else in his place. You can't send someone else to be with the poor. Sending a check is not enough. Jesus says, "I am asking you to go to the poor."

The poor connect us with God. The poor don't just remind us of God; they have the presence of Christ in a substantial way. If you want to be close to God, you should be with the poor. The poor help us love God better.

Whatever you did for the least of my brethren, you did for me.
—MATTHEW 25:37

Jesus made himself a servant of all. We have to get our hands dirty—helping the poor must be personal (e.g., spending time at a homeless shelter). When we face God, we will need a personal letter of recommendation from a poor person.

LISTEN TO YOUR HEART

Jesus says that we are in him, and he is in us. Most of the commandments don't come from Moses—they come from the little voice inside of us. This little voice will guide you; this is the voice of divine guidance. You are always free to ignore the voice—it sometimes tells us things we don't want to hear.

Give the master key of life to God. We let God into parts of our life but deny access to other parts. This requires surrendering to the will of God and placing our trust in God.

The little voice inside you is like having divine GPS in each of us.
—FATHER SCOTT VANDERVEER

In every decision, we should ask, "God, what do you think I should do?" There is one rule of thumb: do the next right thing. Not the easy thing, but the next right thing. Maybe it's making a call to someone that you know you should really call. If we listen to the voice inside of us, we will know how to do the next right thing.

Joy Is an Inside Job

The top regret of the dying is that they didn't allow themselves to be happier. Let's not make that mistake. Choice is a component of happiness—no one makes us mad. We are in charge of our emotions, and our emotions are our responsibility.

On his deathbed, a dying man wrote his obituary: "In lieu of flowers, go out and make people laugh." If you want to have a happy life, sharing and generosity create happiness.

None of us live without regrets—we are not perfect. But we can turn the page and write a new chapter.

Setting the Bar Too Low

When we comply with the Ten Commandments, we are setting the bar really low. We should be aiming so high that it would be impossible to be that good every day. Jesus wants us to reach for a high standard, even if we fail a lot.

> *We should be living our lives for an audience of one and God is the audience.*
> **—MATTHEW KELLY**

God gives us an opportunity to serve every day. Jesus gave a simple commandment: "To love one another as I love you" (John 13:34). This is an extreme commandment because we are called upon to love those who are against us.

Your Unique Destiny

Our call from God is not just to be nice people. We are called to be saints—that is the potential we are called for. God has a specific mission for each of us. Mark Twain said that there are two most important days of your life: the day you are born and

You answer God's call by going one step in the direction of what you are called to do.

the day you find out why. You answer God's call by going one step in the direction of what you are called to do.

We resist God's plan for us; even Jesus wanted to avoid his crucifixion. Be open to the Lord's disruption in your life. The path the Lord wants for you is so much better.

No one would be here on earth without a calling from God.
—FATHER SCOTT VANDERVEER

Jesus did not reveal a big plan—he just took the first step and then took the next step. What are you called to do by God? Can you name the moment when God called you? You do not need to be 100 percent ready for your call from God, just willing.

Time Spent in Prayer

What God wants most from us is quality time with us. Attending church is an hour that God has given us for our growth, and no one can take that from us. Our desire to praise God is, in itself, a gift. Jesus's prayer was, "God, use me—use me however you want."

Listen in silence to God. Be alone and let God talk to you. There can be no prayer without time, just a minute. In silence, God asks us, "What do you want me to do for you?"

Prayer is our best way of speaking with God. God dares us to have a constant conversation with him.
—FATHER SCOTT VANDERVEER

Spending time in prayer is time that God has given to us for our growth, and no one can take that from us. How much time are you willing to give to your soul? Because that is what prayer does.

Are we praying only for our own needs? We are told to forgive one another. Are we praying for that? We should pray for forgiveness and mercy.

Perseverance and Struggle

There is nothing we can go through that Jesus did not experience. There is no one to blame for hardship and struggle. This is so the works of God can be revealed through struggle. The works of God will be visible through us.

Life has struggle; even Jesus was not spared this experience. We have to believe that difficult times are temporary, and if we hold on, the future will be bright. Jesus can't take away the challenges, but he can be with us through them. We have to be a people of hope. We have to persevere in hardships and turmoil.

> *There is no cross that is not followed by a resurrection.*
> **—FATHER SCOTT VANDERVEER**

We will never go through something that God can't handle. There may be many things in life that we cannot handle, but there is nothing that God can't handle. We have to make the decision to turn our lives over to God. The will of God will never take you where the grace of God will not sustain you.

There is nothing worth doing that does not involve struggle. Find a way to offer it up. Pay it forward—as a gift.

Do Not Be Afraid

Jesus's disciples left their homes with no money or possessions and were told that God would take care of their needs. When we are tired, God will support us. If we trust in God, he will provide for our needs.

You are the light of the world. Your light must shine upon others.
—MATTHEW 5:14

All growth happens outside your comfort zone. Being uncomfortable is a sure sign that you are growing.

Radical Forgiveness

There is no limit to God's forgiveness. Peter had a lot of sins. Peter cut off the ear of a guard with a sword (even Jesus's disciples could be violent), he couldn't stay awake for one hour when Jesus needed him, and he denied Jesus three times on the day of Jesus's crucifixion. No one else sinned as much as Peter, but no one loved Jesus more.

We have a clear picture of how far Jesus would go to show love. Peter sinned frequently, but he also loved all the time. Love cancels all sins. We are not defined by our sinfulness but by our love. We are supposed to forgive everyone.

If we can't forgive those who are lost and want to harm us, our faith would be meaningless.
—FATHER SCOTT VANDERVEER

Jesus's willingness to forgive gave us a formula for life. As Jesus was dying on the cross, he said, "Father forgive them. They know not what they do" (Luke 23:34).

> *Jesus taught us, "Sometimes you just need to love the hell out of people."*
> **—FATHER SCOTT VANDERVEER**

Love cancels a multitude of sins.

Mercy and Grace

Everyone who is incarcerated is a child of God. Persons on death row are children of God. God's grace is greater than our flaws and character defects.

> *God's mercy is more powerful than any sin you could have committed.*
> **—FATHER SCOTT VANDERVEER**

God's Love for You

You don't have to spend another moment worrying about how to get God to love you. God's love forces us to be better than we want to be. God's mission is to save us, like Jesus went out of his way to save a tax collector (Luke 19:1).

> *When Jesus thought of you, he thought you*
> *were someone worth dying for.*
> **—FATHER SCOTT VANDERVEER**

Our lives are the only things we can give to God. We may become living sacrifices to God by the lives we live. Focus on sculpting your life into a worthy masterpiece.

The Journey of Life

What matters is the preciousness of the journey. If you focus on the destination, you miss the journey. The journey of life is the gift. A 106-year-old put it aptly: "The secret is to live just one moment at a time."

Forget the past, and focus on what you can do now to change things. What are you being called to do at this moment? Are you prepared for what God is about to do, right here and now?

> *That will always be our choice—what to do in the moment.*
> **—FATHER SCOTT VANDERVEER**

The destination is not where we need to focus. God walks with us on the journey of life. God is here with us, right now and in this moment; we have everything we need.

Give Your Life as a Gift to the World

Whoever is willing to share and give away their life will find it. We are supposed to be giving away our lives. A giver helps people who can't pay them back.

In God's eyes, you are the most precious thing in the world.
—FATHER SCOTT VANDERVEER

Jesus is our model—not to be served but to serve. Jesus pours himself out and shows us the way of a disciple. Let us offer our life to God. What do you want your death to mean for the world? How can your life be a gift for the people you love?

Nurture Relationships

The things that matter most are our relationships. Our relationships with others determines the quality of our lives. The most common deathbed regrets are: (1) I wish I hadn't spent so much time working, (2) I wish I had been able to express my feelings better to those I love, and (3) I wish I had stayed in better touch with others.

Shower the people you love with love.
—JAMES TAYLOR

What are the important relationships in your life? What are your top ten relationships? Is there a beloved aunt or godchild that you haven't spent time with? Can you invest time in that relationship?

Share Your Faith

The courage to lead is a willingness to take risks for the good of an unknown future. What has been the impact of God in your life? Have the courage to share it. Become an expert in the things God has done for you in your life. Share your experiences with God in a humble way, not a preachy one.

> *Jesus said to his disciples, "What I tell you in the darkness, you have to say in the light."*
> **—MATTHEW 10:27**

You are meant to proclaim God's word wherever you go.

> *What I say to you, proclaim on the rooftops. Whoever acknowledges me before others, I will acknowledge before my father.*
> **—MATTHEW 10:32**

We are always moving in a direction in our spiritual life—toward God or toward fear.

> *May we have the courage to proclaim the gospel by the witness of our lives.*
> **—FATHER SCOTT VANDERVEER**

Evangelization is the willingness to engage others in your faith experience. This could be something as simple as discussing your faith experience. It is challenging to talk about faith in mixed company. We should be effusive in our faith and reticent about our opinions.

Being Receptive to the Call of God

Be open. You need to have openness that the next thing that happens to you could be a call from God. If God is calling us and we ignore that call, that would be devastating. If the thief on the cross gives Jesus the power over his life, how much more can we?

Do the work. Doing God's work is labor. When God's call comes, it won't be obvious, and it will be difficult.

> *The tears on your face are the cost of your dreams.*
> **—FATHER SCOTT VANDERVEER**

There will be a cost, and it will be hard. There is no shortcut. There is no way to follow Jesus without self-discipline and sacrifice. You are the only one who can do this.

Ignore the imposter syndrome. You feel that you're not worthy or qualified. Simon Peter said to Jesus, "I'm not worthy. I'm sinful" (Luke 5:8). We are indeed worthy because God made us so. It's not what we think about ourselves that matters—it's what God thinks about us that matters.

> *If you ever doubt how God feels about you, just look at the cross. That's all you have to know.*
> **—FATHER SCOTT VANDERVEER**

The imposter syndrome will stop us from doing what God wants. You are God's only plan for spreading the Gospel.

Confronting Temptation

Hiding from our weaknesses will not work—we have to face them. Name the temptation that you are facing and ask, "What is getting in the way of facing this?"

You can't manage a temptation unless you focus on what matters. If you are tempted by overeating, put a note on the refrigerator that reads, "Nothing tastes as good as being fit feels." Remember what matters most.

Be Humble

We don't need to think less of ourselves—we just need to think of ourselves less. Use all of the opportunities in life to recognize how imperfect we are.

The one who humbles himself will be exalted.
—LUKE 14:11

Difficult Conversations

Having hard conversations is never easy, but when they are rooted in love, you can't mess it up.

Let Go of Resentment

It takes effort to hold onto resentment—you hold onto the hurt. When you hold onto resentment, something dies within you. You should pray for those who have wronged you.

The Meaning of Death

No one wants to die. We think of death as the worst thing, but it is the only entrance to our true home. The number-one fear is the fear of dying, but that is the only way to eternal life. We are afraid of the very thing that is the cornerstone of our faith.

Heaven is like a king who hosts a magnificent banquet, and the joy is extreme. Paul said, "For me, death is gain. I long to depart this world and be with Christ" (Philippians 1:19). Teresa of Avila said, "Heaven is being in the presence of God."

Heaven is being in God's presence and knowing that you are.
—FATHER SCOTT VANDERVEER

God did not bring us this far to leave us. Those who die go to be with God.

We are all going to die someday. God has never promised to save us from dying. God did not save Jesus from dying. Jesus did not come to save us from dying; he came to save us from death.

Don't worry about death. God made us imperishable. When a twelve-year-old-girl died, Jesus said to her mother, "Don't be afraid. Just have faith" (Mark 5:36). In death, life has changed, not ended. At death, you will see that God's wonderful promises are true.

Doing Your Best

We are always asked by God to do the very best we can do. What good does it do to dwell on the past? Making mistakes is the price of being human. God has chosen a way to help us learn by making mistakes.

God grant me the serenity to accept the things I can't change. Give me the courage to change the things I can. And give me wisdom to know the difference.
—THE SERENITY PRAYER

Life is not like a train—it is more like a sailboat, in which the wind continually changes and you have to adjust the route.

Compassion for the Weak

When you show compassion to a stranger in need, you are living the message of Jesus. We should love our neighbors, even when they are not like us at all. Who have we walked by and not helped?

> *Anything worth doing is going to involve struggle.*
> **—FATHER SCOTT VANDERVEER**

God asks us to help everyone, regardless of who they are.

Confronting Doubt

Do you ever wonder if it is all true? Many people have doubt, no matter how much they believe—that's part of faith. Even after all that they had seen Jesus do, the apostles had doubt (Matthew 28:17). Faith is believing in things that you cannot see.

We want to believe that we have perfect faith, but like "doubting Thomas" (John 20:24), there is so much we don't understand. Thomas spent three years living with Jesus and witnessed many miracles, but he still had difficulty believing.

> *For faith to be faith, there must be some risk involved. Doubts are a beautiful part of faith.*
> **—FATHER SCOTT VANDERVEER**

When you have doubt, fix your heart on the amazing things God has done for you. Stay focused on what God has done for you.

Measuring Backward

When you are facedown on the floor, the best thing you can do is look back and see how far you've come.

Forgive Yourself

Jesus has already died for the sins of the world, so you don't have to feel shame for your sins. If God could have made you any better, he would have. Each of us is more than the worst things we've done. Focusing on your sins is not the best way to measure how strong your faith is.

When asked to condemn an adulterer, Jesus immediately forgives her (Luke 7:36). In a few days, Jesus will forgive his own murder. God can forgive any sin. You are forbidden to feel guilty for your sins because God has already forgiven them. There is a distinction between who we are and what we've done.

God made you, and God doesn't make junk.
—FATHER SCOTT VANDERVEER

The question is: What do we do with that forgiveness? What are we supposed to do with our shame? All of us are imperfect with character defects. Our flaws bring about God's glory.

Hope for the Future

God did not send his son into the world to condemn the world, but to save the world.
—JOHN 3:16

Jesus transformed our future from one of fear to one of hope.

Thank you, Father Scott VanDerveer, for being the source of this content. You have inspired and transformed lives and deepened our faith and trust in God. I am grateful to call you my friend.

FAMILY

The quality of our relationships determines the quality of our lives.

—ESTHER PEREL

CHAPTER 20:

WHAT IT MEANS TO BE IRISH

As I sat in the kitchen of the doctor's home at five thirty in the morning, I was struck by the thought that the doctor and I had nothing in common. The doctor and I had gotten along just fine during our meeting at his home, but aside from our work together on a medical malpractice lawsuit, we could not have been more different.

The doctor, in his midsixties, was a friendly, engaging cardiologist from Tampa, and his palatial lakeside home had artwork and other remnants of his Jewish heritage throughout the house. Sitting across from the doctor was a Catholic lawyer who knew little about the Jewish religion, other than a limited knowledge of Hebrew scripture. The doctor did not share my passion for sports, nor did I share his interest in Jewish art and cultural artifacts. From anyone's point of view, the lawyer and doctor were two strangers whose lives had just happened to cross paths.

A Shocking Revelation

As I sat at the kitchen counter eating a bowl of cereal, the doctor asked, just to make small talk, where I had gone to law school. I glanced in the direction of the doctor and casually mentioned, "Notre Dame." A few seconds passed with no response from the doctor, and I eventually looked up to be met by an incredulous expression on his face. The doctor's eyebrows pointed up, his mouth was wide open, and for a moment or two, he seemed incapable of speech. It was as though the doctor had just spotted Bigfoot standing behind me.

The doctor eventually explained that his only daughter—a New York City corporate lawyer—had also graduated from Notre Dame Law School. OK, I thought, this was a surprise coming from a Jewish cardiologist but not exactly earth shattering ... until the doctor explained.

A Unique College Student

The doctor's daughter had been first in her class at the University of Virginia and had her pick of any of the elite Ivy League law schools. Notre Dame Law School wasn't on her radar. But the doctor's daughter wasn't your typical scholar—she couldn't speak or hear.

The doctor's daughter faced subtle forms of discrimination in college. As a deaf student, the doctor's daughter had to read lips to understand classroom lectures, and on occasion, male professors refused to shave the facial hair covering their lips. Just being able to understand the lectures of male professors with beards or mustaches was a challenge. The doctor's daughter accepted her professors' indifference to her deafness by striving harder in her studies.

By the fall of her senior year, the doctor's daughter was ranked first in her class, and her future was bright. The doctor's daughter had been accepted into top Ivy League law schools, and she had her pick of any of the top five law schools. Then a TV morning show changed everything.

How a TV Morning Show Changed Everything

During an early morning of her senior year, the doctor's daughter happened to turn on the TV to a morning show about a story of the valedictorian at Notre Dame. But this story had a special twist: Notre Dame's valedictorian was not your typical college student—he was blind.

The TV program featured stories of the challenges facing the valedictorian and the special accommodations made at Notre Dame by the administration, professors, and classmates to help him overcome the enormous obstacles facing a blind student. And the results were amazing—he finished first in his class and, for perhaps the first time ever, a blind student was accepted to medical school.

When the TV story was over, the doctor's daughter knew where she would go to law school. If Notre Dame was willing to make these over-the-top accommodations for a disabled undergrad, it was the perfect place for her. A difficult decision was made easy.

An Unlikely Subway Alumnus

Following his daughter's admission to Notre Dame Law School, the doctor began visiting the campus and taking in the traditions that are unique to the Fighting Irish. The doctor began going to Notre Dame for football weekends, and after immersing himself in the culture and traditions, he became a raving member of Notre Dame's subway alumni.

The doctor sang the alma mater on flights to South Bend for football games, and I could hardly get him to stop talking about his love of the university. As it turns out, the doctor's collection of Notre Dame paraphernalia was almost as impressive as his collection of Jewish art and cultural remnants. Someone whom you would least expect to be associated with Notre Dame turned out to be one of its biggest fans.

What It Means to Be Irish

Being Irish is not about a degree, and it's not about spending four years on campus. Being Irish means having a love for Notre Dame—a love that you hesitate to share with anyone outside of the Notre Dame family for fear that you will be considered obnoxious and self-centered. Your heart beats faster when you meet another ND fan—alumnus or not—and in the right company, you don't hesitate to share your special feelings for Our Lady's university.

Being Irish is not about a degree, and it's not about spending four years on campus. Being Irish means having a love for Notre Dame.

Perhaps more than anything else, it is Notre Dame's unique ability to capture the heart and soul of just about anyone—regardless of faith or religion—and transform them into members of the Notre Dame family. And every once in a while, you run into a member of the Notre

Dame family when it is least expected … like a business meeting over breakfast with a Jewish cardiologist.

A Special Christmas Dream Come True

Eight years ago, I got a call on my way home from work from my nineteen-year-old nephew, Peter Ryan. Peter gave me the news that everyone in our family had been praying for—he had been accepted to Notre Dame! Peter was the fourth generation of my family to call Notre Dame home, and I can't think of anything that would have made my father, James H. Fisher (class of '58) or grandfather, Henry Fisher (class of '34), prouder.

In the 1993 movie *Rudy*, the best friend of Rudy Ruettiger, tells him to pursue his dream to play football at Notre Dame by encouraging him, saying, "Having dreams is what makes life tolerable."

Rudy's best friend was right: dreams are what make life worth living. Thank you, Notre Dame, for making another dream come true.

—John H. Fisher ('88, '91 Law)

CHAPTER 21:

FAMILIES ARE CHOSEN, NOT BORN

BY TIM FISHER (HIS COLLEGE ESSAY)

For centuries, the traditional definition of a family is a group of persons with common ancestors and DNA, but in my view, that is an incomplete definition. I am living proof that a family is not born; it is chosen.

On July 28, 1999, a twin boy and girl were born in a small town in Russia. The twins are my sister, Liliya, and me. Four months earlier, on April 2, another boy, Alek, was born nearby. Through a series of events that could not have been predicted, my sister, brother, and I were brought to the United States on October 30, 2000. My parents adopted the three of us, and the roots of a new family were planted. Families are chosen, not born.

Since being adopted, I have lived seventeen years with my family. Through good and bad times, my parents have supported me, along with my grandparents, aunts, uncles, and the other members of my extended *family*. Although we are not related by common ancestors or DNA, it has been love that binds my adoptive family and me. It is our love that makes a family *my* family.

It was not until I was older that I began to understand that Alek has mental disabilities, including developmental disabilities caused by fetal alcohol syndrome. Alek's speech can be hard to understand, his handwriting is difficult to read, and he often struggles to make friends and fit in at school.

Alek forgets things, and on occasion it can be frustrating. But even when I get frustrated, I never forget that Alek is my brother, and I love him. When classmates make fun of or bully Alek, I am the first to stick up for him. Even though we are not bound by common ancestors or DNA, it is our love that binds us as brothers, as family.

The motto for my varsity high school soccer team is "United We Are One." Before every game, my coach and the members of the team stress the importance of family, and we eat dinner together. I have never before been on a team that felt like family.

On other teams, I would be forced to the practice squad and be left with the sense that I was not as important as the better players. But with my soccer team, I feel welcome—everyone feels welcome. Although the members of our soccer team came together from different towns, cultures, and even different parts of the world, we love and respect each other, and our bond brings us together as a group, a team, a soccer family.

Family does not only consist of your ancestors—that is an incomplete definition of family. Your family consists of the persons whom you love, protect, and would die for.

Family does not only consist of your ancestors—that is an incomplete definition of family. Your family consists of the persons whom you love, protect, and would die for. Just like my parents chose me, I am choosing my family now.

* * *

A Father's Tribute to His Little Peanut
(Liliya Fisher, 2021 Fordham Alumna)

Lily,

On this special day (May 19, 2021), my heart fills with pride.

Our little peanut (and my angel) walks up on a stage to receive her degree at a prestigious university. But today is much more than a ceremony.

You put in the work—not only in college, but throughout high school, junior high school, and elementary. You worked hard to always do your best and, in doing so, made Mom and I proud.

On the day before graduation, we learned that you received an A and A- in two of your final classes at Fordham, and the GPA in your major will be even higher than 3.71. This is an accomplishment of hard work. I take great pride in telling anyone who will listen that my little girl is an honors student at Fordham. My eyes tear up in pride as I write this.

You became a Division 1 athlete—not through natural ability or talent but through sheer hard work. Rising every morning six days a week for crew reflects your dedication to your crewmates and your hard work and resolve. These qualities will serve you well throughout your life.

You never forget to tell Mom and I (and your brothers) that you love us. You made it a point to call Mom and I and, on occasion, come home to see us. Your family knows you love us because you made the effort to show us.

Throughout your life, there will always be others with more talent and ability, but there is one thing they won't have: your work ethic and motivation to succeed. Hard work and your motivation to succeed will get you much further in life than intelligence or natural ability. The hard workers always win.

You are a kind and gentle young lady. Always strive to be kind and respect those less fortunate than yourself. Your service to the less fortunate (e.g., the homeless and disabled) will make your life special.

Strive to build your relationship with God. Spend time in thought and prayer. God wants nothing more than your time. Show God you care.

Do not take a single day for granted. Time is precious. Treat every moment of life as the precious gift that it is.

Never forget to call your brothers, mother, and me just to say hi and tell us that you love us. Know that we love you dearly, even when you are far away.

Today, the rest of the audience will see a young lady receive her diploma on a stage. That is only a small part of the picture. I see my daughter, who worked hard, faced challenges head on, struggled at times, and ultimately persevered. And my heart swells with pride.

October 24, 2000, will always be the most special day of our lives. On that special day, God gave us the most special gift of our lives: a precious baby girl and her brothers. On this day, I am reminded of how far you've come and how proud I am.

Keep working hard, strive to persevere over challenges, and never stop believing in yourself. And always know Mom and I will be your biggest fans as long as we live.

May God bless you. I love you, Liliya,

Dad
May 19, 2021
Bronx, New York

* * *

Graduation Day, December 16, 2021

(Timothy B. Fisher, 2021 Clemson alumnus)

Tim,

On your graduation day, Mom and I are proud of you.

Proud—not only because of your success and graduation from a prestigious university—but because you are an honest man. You have a quality that is indispensable to success—namely, integrity. This quality will serve you well throughout your life, both professionally and personally.

Always strive to do the right thing. This will not be easy. When others tell small lies, tell the truth. When others try to convince you that you can take a shortcut, ignore them. Be true to yourself, and your character will serve you well throughout life. Integrity is the most important quality that a person can have.

Don't let a day go by without taking a small step to improve yourself. Commit to learning something new every day—read a passage from scripture or Shakespeare. Expand your mind, and take advantage of the wisdom contained in literature and self-improvement books and classes.

Warren Buffett once said that his greatest investment was taking the Dale Carnegie course. Improving yourself is the best investment you will ever make.

Be brave, take chances, and carve out a future that is big and bold. And as long as we are alive, Mom and I will be your biggest fans, but you must begin making your future today.

God bless you, Tim. I love you.

Dad
December 16, 2021
Clemson, South Carolina

PROFESSIONAL / GOAL SETTING

All achievement, no matter what may be its purpose, must begin with an intense, burning desire for something definite.
—**NAPOLEON HILL**, Think and Grow Rich

CHAPTER 22:

THE BEST LESSON A FATHER CAN GIVE HIS SON

This was a lesson that I would never forget.

During a summer gig working as a grunt at Shearson Lehman Brothers in NYC in 1987, I overheard stockbrokers talking about copper as an investment, and I became intrigued. A fan of investing, I spent time studying everything I could about copper from supply and demand and mining and distribution from remote countries such as Zambia and Chile. After a couple of months of research as a neophyte investor, I gradually became convinced that the price of copper was ready to soar.

Friends and family urged me to avoid the temptation to invest in copper. At first I listened to their well-intentioned advice, but after a few months of fighting the temptation, I just couldn't resist.

A Neophyte Investor Makes a Bold Gamble

From my college dorm room in the fall of 1987, I opened an investment account with Shearson Lehman Brothers and deposited my life savings (three months of savings from my summer job) of two thousand dollars. I had clear and specific instructions for my stockbroker: invest all of my hard-earned cash into a commodities option known as a "call." A commodities call option is a kind of bet with long odds that rarely pays off. If copper made a big spike in price within two to three months, I might make a few dollars, but otherwise, I would lose all of my money. The odds were stacked against me.

After taking the dive into commodities options, I did what most college students would do: I woke up at 5:30 a.m. Monday through Friday to buy the *Wall Street Journal* so that I could check the price of copper (the internet didn't exist). Almost to my amazement, the price of copper continued to rise. Days, weeks, and then months passed with the price of copper on a steady upward path, and with every new increase in the price, I counted a fat paper profit in my head. Just maybe I wasn't crazy.

With just a few days left until the option expired, I was forced to sell. When the option was sold, my investment account had ten thousand dollars. I turned a two-thousand-dollar investment into ten thousand and made a 400 percent return on my investment in only three months. For a college student with only a few dollars in his wallet, this was heady stuff … and the worst possible thing that could have happened.

The Worst Thing That Could Have Happened

I was now convinced that I had the Midas touch, and I began investing on margin (loan) in speculative currency options, such as the Japanese yen and Swiss franc. Things went south quickly. My account value dwindled by the day, and I soon realized I had made a huge mistake.

While hanging out in my dorm room on a Friday afternoon, I got a phone call from my stockbroker with scary news. There was a "margin call," on my account and I had to deposit an additional one thousand dollars into it, or the account would be liquidated. I stood to lose all of the four thousand dollars in my account.

A Story with a Surprise Ending

As a college student with no job, I didn't have one thousand dollars—or even fifteen dollars—and I only had one option: call my dad and beg for help. When I placed the call, I was relieved when my dad answered the phone on a late afternoon on a Friday. I explained my quandary and apologized profusely for my stupidity. I promised my dad that if he would deposit one thousand dollars into my account, I would sell the commodities options, return his money, and stop investing in commodities. I explained that this would allow me to keep the four thousand dollars, and I would never ignore his advice again.

My dad quickly responded with "Good luck" and hung up the phone. I was dumbfounded when I heard the click on the other end of the phone. I was flat out of luck—this was my only chance to save my investment. I never heard from the stockbroker again, my account was liquidated, and I lost every penny.

A Priceless Lesson from Dad

At the time, this made no sense, but in hindsight, it makes perfect sense. My dad knew then what I didn't know: *I had to stand on my own two feet and survive without anyone's help.* I could not rely on Mommy or Daddy to get me out of trouble for even another day—I had to fend for myself.

> **Losing four thousand dollars meant nothing. But the lesson that my dad taught me was priceless.**

My dad could have told me these things, but it wouldn't have been the same. This lesson made me tougher, stronger, and most importantly, self-reliant. In hindsight, losing four thousand dollars meant nothing. But the lesson that my dad taught me was priceless.

Thanks, Dad, for the best lesson a father can give his son. I love and miss you.

CHAPTER 23:

WHY LAWSUITS MATTER

It was during a dark, freezing night in December when I made a spur-of-the-moment decision to drive the long way home. As I drove home down a rural road in the middle of nowhere, I approached an industrial plant that was well known to me. The industrial plant was the site of a number of collisions between trains and tractor trailers at its entrance, several of which had resulted in death and horrible injuries for the truckers.

As I began to pass the industrial plant, I spotted something out of the corner of my eye: a temporary booth about the size of a portable toilet in front of the entrance to the plant. Intrigued by this new booth at the entrance, I pulled to the side of the road, got out of my car, and began walking toward the booth.

As I got to within a couple of hundred feet, a uniformed "cop" came rushing out of the booth, pointed a flashlight in my direction, and, showing no courtesy for a stranger, shouted, "Get lost!" (using more

It dawned on me for the first time: *years of work weren't wasted.*

colorful words). As I turned around and began walking back to my car, it dawned on me for the first time: *years of work weren't wasted.*

The Dark, Ugly Secret of an Industrial Plant

The entrance to the industrial plant had a long, dark history. Collisions between trains and tractor trailers at the grade crossing at the entrance to the industrial plant were not uncommon: over the course of eight years, there were nine collisions involving freight trains colliding into tractor trailers at the entrance (the average grade crossing has one wreck every thirty-one years). The federal Department of Transportation had classified the grade crossing as the most dangerous crossing in New York State for over thirty years.

For more than twenty-five years, one meeting after another had been held between the plant's owner, the railroad, and the town and county to fix the problem. There was an obvious danger to truckers (with three truck-train collisions in only three weeks), but the politicians, plant, and railroad were all talk, no action, and no one wanted to take responsibility or pay to fix the problem. Truckers were getting horribly injured, with devastating brain and orthopedic injuries, and dying, but no changes were made to the grade crossing.

Very predictably, the train-truck collisions resulted in a rash of lawsuits against the plant, railroad, and municipalities. I handled three of the cases on behalf of truckers and the estate of a trucker, and truth be told, it wasn't hard. The paper trail left by the bureaucrats showed innumerable meetings with no tangible evidence of any changes to the grade crossing. This was a plaintiffs' lawyer's dream come true.

A Hard Reality for an Idealistic Young Lawyer

Eventually there was a price to pay. After throwing all of their resources into fighting the lawsuits, hiring the most expensive defense lawyers and expert witnesses, and taking the first few lawsuits to trial, the industrial plant, railroad, and the municipalities realized they were fighting a losing battle. The lawsuits were settled once the plant, railroad, and municipalities realized they couldn't win—they had ignored a serious danger at the grade crossing for way too long.

As the cases were settled and I began moving on to other work, I became disillusioned. After years of hard work and substantial settlements, nothing changed—the grade crossing remained exactly the same way that it had for more than thirty years. It was just a matter of time until more truckers were horribly injured and killed, and I was troubled by the realization that the lawsuits hadn't done a thing to make the grade crossing safer.

Perhaps I was realizing for the first time in my career that sometimes lawsuits don't make a bit of difference. An idealistic young lawyer was confronting a hard reality.

Proof That Lawsuits Make a Difference

Then, on a dark, cold winter night on a rural county road, I saw with my own eyes the impact that lawsuits can have. For the first time in more than thirty years, the railroad had hired a crossing guard to stop traffic when trains were crossing the grade crossing. The problem had a simple fix—namely, an unskilled, minimum-wage crossing guard whose only job was to stop traffic whenever trains approached the grade crossing. Problem solved! There would be no more injuries and no more lawsuits.

But the story gets better. About a quarter-mile up the road, construction was taking place to build a new entrance to the industrial plant and relocate the grade crossing. About a year later, the new entrance that was open for traffic had a unique feature: it was one of the safest grade crossings in the country.

And as for the old grade crossing, it was shut down and permanently closed.

The most dangerous grade crossing in New York State was replaced by one of the safest. It wasn't easy, and tragically, way too much blood was spilled over years of inaction and indifference, but eventually the problem was fixed by bureaucrats, a railroad, and a plant that refused to confront a harsh reality … until lawsuits forced them to.

The Next Time You Hear a Lawyer Joke …

The next time you hear someone make a lawyer joke, don't tell them that you're insulted or that they're wrong. Tell them your own story about how lawsuits change lives and make everyone safer. Tell them about a grade crossing that went from being the most dangerous to one of the safest. Share with them a story about overcoming bureaucratic indifference to public safety and how lawsuits can force corporations and municipalities to fix dangerous hazards.

Don't be surprised by their response; the public bias against injury law is too strong. There's a good chance they'll listen politely, nod their head to be polite, and subtly find a way to leave your company. That's understandable because few people have seen for themselves the impact that lawsuits can make.

But it's OK to be idealistic on occasion and enjoy a reminder of the power that lawsuits can have ... just like I did during a drive home on a country road on a cold winter night.

* * *

Lessons from My First Trial

Sitting alone at the plaintiffs' counsel table in the courtroom (and trying to act as though I knew what I was doing), the trial was about to begin. With sweaty palms and a sweat-drenched back, I felt fears and doubts racing through my mind. I thought, *Am I really the right lawyer to be doing this?*

I quickly shot a glance over at the counsel table for the defense. Hunkering together and strategizing for my defeat were three much older, far more experienced defense lawyers with thousand-dollar suits, who seemed ready to feast on a young, inexperienced lawyer (me). I tried reassuring myself that I'd be OK, as a senior partner at my law firm was supposed to show up to the courtroom and help with the trial. Turns out, help never arrived.

Moments later, the judge asked for the opening statement of the plaintiffs. I glanced back to see if the senior partner of my law firm had arrived, but the back of the courtroom was empty. I got up and did the only thing I could think of: I told the story of a paralyzed, brain-damaged baby who never should have ended up that way.

When opening statements were finished during a recess, a young defense lawyer who had been observing the trial made a hand gesture indicating he wanted to speak with me. The young defense lawyer put his hand against the side of his mouth and whispered, almost apologetically, "I know I'm not supposed to say this ... but you gave the best opening statement I've ever heard."

That was the beginning of my first trial.

The Indoctrination of a Young, Clueless Lawyer

Over the next week and a half of the trial, I worked day and night to review medical records, organize exhibits and deposition transcripts, meet with witnesses, and prepare expert witnesses for their testimony. Turns out, my star expert witness had not taken his Xanax and made threats to leave town without testifying. Sleep was limited to four hours a night, but even then, sleep was limited by an anxiety-ridden mind concerned about what could go wrong.

Almost to my amazement, things seemed to be going OK. The testimony of our witnesses went well, exhibits were admitted into evidence, and while our star expert witness took some lumps on cross examination, it could have been worse. Each day was a new challenge, and I convinced myself to keep going.

On the eighth day of the trial, the defense decided they had had enough and settled the case. The settlement would cover the costs of raising a severely handicapped little girl for the rest of her life. In the mind of a young, inexperienced lawyer, justice had been served.

A Juror Gets the Last Word

After the jurors had been informed about the settlement, one of them lingered around the courtroom and asked to speak with me. The juror told me that he'd had little respect for trial lawyers or personal injury law before the trial, but after seeing a trial firsthand, he told me that his view had changed completely.

The juror told me that he respected what we do and that he now realized that our system makes a difference for the disabled. As he walked out of the courtroom, the juror turned back in my direction and told me he was grateful he had gotten the chance to serve on the jury.

And that is what the public never gets to see.

* * *

What My Dad Taught Me about the Practice of Law

While waiting around in the hallway of a cramped courthouse in Kingston, New York, a male in his midsixties heard my last name and asked, "Are you Jimmy Fisher's son?"

When I responded affirmatively, this man proceeded to tell me a story that I will never forget. This man had a lawsuit in which James H. Fisher, Esq., had represented his adversary in a boundary line dispute involving real estate. This man did not have a lawyer in this lawsuit (a pro se litigant) and tried to manage the legal system the best that he could, but he was at a clear disadvantage.

During this lawsuit, my father's client wanted to take advantage of the opposing party's vulnerability as a pro se litigant. Rather than taking advantage of the fact that the opposing side did not have legal representation, my father advised his client that he was being unreasonable and convinced him to agree upon settlement terms that were fair for both sides.

My father, James H. Fisher, Esq., could have taken advantage of a pro se litigant, but he knew that wasn't the right thing to do. As a result, the case was settled on terms that were fair, and the pro se litigant was left with a memory that he wanted to share with anyone who would listen—specifically, that lawyers are good people and, while imperfect like everyone else, they try to do the right thing.

> **Lawyers are good people and, while imperfect like everyone else, they try to do the right thing.**

There's never a bad time to do the right thing. That is the best thing that I learned about practice of law from my dad, James H. Fisher, Esq., and it's a lesson that I will carry with me forever.

* * *

The Most Difficult Decision that a Lawyer Will Ever Have to Make

It was the first day of jury selection. Before jury selection begins the prospective jurors complete a juror questionnaire about their age, family and employment status. On the jury questionnaire, three members of the jury panel shared that they were Jehovah's Witness members.

During the first break in jury selection, defense counsel asked to speak with the Judge. In the courtroom, defense counsel told the judge that she had encountered Jehovah's Witnesses during previous jury selections and in her view, they were not appropriate for jury service based upon their religious views. Specifically, defense counsel explained that it is well known that Jehovah's Witnesses place God's law before the law given to them by the Judge.

In a sarcastic tone, the judge rhetorically asked, "What is God's law anyway?" I asked the Judge to speak with the Jehovah's Witness members to inquire about potential biases and determine for herself whether they were appropriate for jury service. The judge declined my request and stated that the Jehovah's Witness members were not appropriate for jury service. The judge dismissed the three Jehovah's Witnesses from jury service, even though some of them had not been questioned by the lawyers or judge.

After their dismissal, a thirty-seven-year-old male, one of the Jehovah's Witness members, approached me. This man shared that he viewed it as his civic duty to serve on a jury and he was disappointed that he would not get the chance. This man acknowledged that he would always place God's law before anything else, but he could conceive of no circumstances in the medical malpractice trial where such a conflict might occur.

This man, his wife, and another Jehovah's Witness member were sent home and not permitted to be a member of a jury. Even months after this occurred, I am still stunned.

Following the trial, I had a decision to make. I could ignore what happened during jury selection, or I could file a formal complaint against the judge. Without question, the easier path was to do nothing.

Filing a formal complaint against a judge is not good for a lawyer's career. I knew that there would likely be harsh consequences, not only from the judge, but also from the judge's colleagues in the small county (Putnam County, New York) where the discrimination occurred. But I knew that ignoring discrimination was not an option. There was really no choice to be made, so I filed the formal complaint against the judge.

What happened next was not entirely surprising. For the first time in my career, I was sanctioned by a judge and I had to pay $7,500 for my "misconduct." I paid the fine and appealed the judge's order to New York's Appellate Division. I am confident that justice will be served by the higher court and, most importantly, that the judge's discrimination will be exposed.

It is irrelevant which religious group faced the discrimination. I would have done the same thing whether the discrimination was against Hindus, Muslims, Sikhs, or atheists. The religious views of the prospective jurors do not matter. What matters is that the courtroom was closed to three members of a particular faith and I could not look the other way.

During the commencement speech for law school, the dean of our law school told us that we were not becoming a "Notre Dame lawyer" on that day. The dean explained that each one of us would eventually face the most difficult ethical decision of our career. We would be forced to choose between an easy path of doing nothing or the difficult path of doing the right thing, even knowing that there would be harsh consequences. And on the day when we made the difficult ethical choice, only then would we be a "Notre Dame lawyer".

On that day, I wasn't quite sure what the dean meant ... but now I do.

CHAPTER 24:

THREE SIMPLE STEPS FOR MAKING DREAMS COME TRUE

Writing your dreams on paper increases the likelihood that you will achieve them. A goal-setting study by Dominican University in 1979 showed that prior to graduation,

- eighty-four percent of the class had no goals at all,
- thirteen percent of the class had set written goals but had no concrete plans, and
- three percent of the class had both written goals and concrete plans.

Ten years later, the 13 percent of the class that had set written goals but had not created plans were making twice as much money as the 84 percent of the class that had set no goals at all.

However, the 3 percent of the class that had both written goals and a plan were making ten times as much as the rest of the 97 percent of the class. Lesson learned: *To achieve your goals, they need to be written out and planned for.* Without a plan, chances for success are minimal.

Become a dream maker by following these three simple steps:

Step 1: Document Your Top Dreams

Write down your top goals, and add a specific date for completion of the goals.

By January 18, 2023, I will

- weigh 163.6 pounds or less;

- finish my third book, *Win Today*;

- retain three catastrophic injury, non-medical-malpractice cases;

- expand the Mastermind Experience to Santa Monica, California;

- run a marathon;

- launch my coaching program for lawyers;

- hire a full-time marketing director; and

- take Lisa and our kids to Russia.

Step 2: Create a Plan of Action for Your Top Goal

Circle the top goal that you want to achieve. I circled "launch my coaching program for lawyers." Next, list the key things you will do to achieve that goal.

- Finish the "shock and awe" for referring lawyers.
- Create a website for the coaching program.
- Document the policies and systems for the coaching program.
- Hire a mentor for the coaching program.
- Expand and define the benefits of the coaching program.
- Hold accountability sessions with accountability partner.
- Accumulate testimonials from lawyers.
- Add testimonials to the coaching website.
- Create e-commerce platform to accept payments.

Step 3: Get an Accountability Partner

Dreams and plans are a great start, but the odds are stacked against you without accountability. A study by Statistic Brain showed that most dreamers don't get far before quitting:

- Seventy-five percent made it through the first week.
- Seventy-one percent made it past two weeks.
- Sixty-four percent made it past one month.
- Forty-six percent made it past six months.

Sharing your goals with an accountability partner will keep you accountable. Set regular (daily or weekly) accountability phone calls to check in with your partner and report on your effort level. This will virtually guarantee your success because you won't want to report that you've done nothing.

> **Dreams and plans are a great start, but the odds are stacked against you without accountability.**

And *take action*, even if it is a small step. Little actions lead to big results (and dreams that come true).

* * *

Staying Positive by Measuring Backward

We all have an ideal vision of our future and set lofty goals, but when you look into the future, you'll always be disappointed. When you measure forward, you will be thinking of the things you haven't achieved, no matter how far you've come. You'll be disheartened by how far you have to go because your future goals are constantly moving targets.

MEASURE BACKWARD

Instead, *measure backward*. Look back to where you began, and measure from the point where you are now to see how far you've gone. You will be shocked and amazed at the enormous gains you've made, sometimes in only three to six months.

Think of the accomplishments you've had only in the past three months, and take a few minutes to write them down. Now share them with a friend or family member. Trust me, you'll feel a lot better once you've done this. You'll realize you've come a long way, and you'll reflect back with pride at your accomplishments.

THE MOST POSITIVE TOOL FOR YOUR MINDSET

Why does *measuring backward* work? This mindset instills a sense of accomplishment, increases your confidence, and is a new way of viewing your past and setting goals.

You might write down your accomplishments in a gratitude journal. And when you're feeling down or discouraged, read through your gratitude journal, and reflect back on how far you've come. You'll feel damn good after doing this.

Measuring backward is the most powerful tool taught by Dan Sullivan at Strategic Coach. We know measuring backward will work for you.

CHAPTER 25:

WHY FAILURE IS ESSENTIAL TO SUCCESS

Make a decision, and then change course if it ends up being wrong. Make decisions with 70 percent of the information you wish you had. Stop waiting until you have everything you wish you had to make a decision; you're wasting time.
—JEFF BEZOS, JANUARY 3, 2018

In 1995, Jeff Bezos had an idea to build a business based upon "online commerce." The growth of the internet would be the key to Bezos's success.

- When Jeff Bezos first broached his business idea with his parents, his father asked, "What's the internet?"
- Bezos borrowed $300,000 from his parents and additional funds from friends to launch Amazon.
- In 1995, Amazon had five employees (almost all software coders).

- During the first few years, Amazon operated out of a strip mall in a small office.

- During the financial collapse in 1998, Amazon's stock price lost more than 90 percent of its value by dropping from $113 per share to $6 per share.

- Most of the software companies in Silicon Valley went broke during the dot-com bubble in 1998.

- Amazon created a smartphone (Fire) that was an epic failure and lost $178 million.

- With a capital value worth almost $2 trillion, Amazon continues to work with the "Day One" mindset of frugality and creativity (Amazon's main office building is called "Day One").

- Amazon continues to take chances that lose billions of dollars.

In 2022, Jeff Bezos was the wealthiest person in the world.

The concept that played the biggest factor in Bezos's success? *Successful failure.* Taking risks, making mistakes, losing money, and refining Amazon's processes with a singular focus—namely, obsession with the customer.

Taking risks, making mistakes, and getting better are lessons for all of us. And they are essential to success.

***

How a Friendly Smile Can Change Everything

How you treat people determines your success.

During my first five years out of law school, I represented the Subway sandwich company in their disputes with problem franchises (e.g., franchises that did not pay their franchise fees or had problems with their landlord). I could always tell whether a franchisee would succeed or fail by one thing: Did the owner greet you with a smile when you met them for the first time?

If the owner greets you with a smile (and ideally calls you by name and acts like they are happy to see you), I know the franchise will succeed. If the owner has a flat personality and simply greets you with the perfunctory, "How can I help you?" I can virtually guarantee the owner will fail.

It's really that simple. Your business will not succeed or fail based upon the quality of your service or product. It's a given that you're good at what you do. A smile combined with a "How are you doing, my friend?" goes a long way and, over the long haul, virtually guarantees success for an owner of any business.

The Key to Success

How you treat people determines your success.

The next time you walk into a store, focus on whether the owner (or their employees) greets you with a smile. If not, the business won't be there for long.

Your success in life is not determined by your intelligence, where you went to school, or your analytical abilities. Success is determined by something much simpler: how you treat people.

Does it seem counterintuitive that such a simple thing determines success? Perhaps, but your ability to engage your customers and clients and treat them with respect and an occasional smile is more important than anything else. I'm willing to bet that the troubled franchise owners at Subway might tell you—in hindsight—the same thing.

Professionally and personally, nothing has had a bigger impact on my life than Dale Carnegie training. If you ever get a chance to recommend Dale Carnegie training to a family member or friend, don't hesitate (or maybe foot the bill). Nothing is more powerful in changing your life.

But don't take my word for this. When asked about his greatest investment, the wealthiest person in the world, Warren Buffett, responded, "Dale Carnegie training."

* * *

You Were Meant for Greatness

It's easy to think that we are not meant to do great things. Sometimes those who know us try to lower our expectations of what is possible and make us more "realistic." Ignore these people.

God created each one of us to accomplish amazing things. You were meant to live an incredible life. When your friends or colleagues tell you that you can only accomplish so much, what they are really doing is trying to get you to live down to their standards. Don't listen to them.

In the winter Olympics in Lake Placid in 1980, the US hockey team was told that they had no chance of beating the greatest team in the world from the Soviet Union. The pundits wrote off the US hockey team—all except for the coach and his players. The US hockey players and their coach were the only ones who believed that they would beat the Soviet Union, and without that belief, the greatest upset in sports history would not have been possible.

You, too, were born to accomplish incredible things. Listen to those who inspire and motivate you to accomplish great things, and ignore the naysayers. Great accomplishments will always be within your grasp as long as you never quit.

SACRIFICE AND GENEROSITY

What we have done for ourselves dies with us; what we have done for others and the world remains and is immortal.

—ALBERT PIKE

CHAPTER 26:

A LIFE WORTHY OF RESPECT

When I was a young boy, a homeless person, known to most as the "Birdman," in my hometown of Kingston, New York, came to my church for Mass on Sunday mornings. The Birdman always sat in the front pew, and he wore multiple layers of dirty, tattered clothes.

Few parishioners sat near the Birdman during Mass, and few had the courage to go anywhere near him. When the Birdman sat in his usual spot in the front pew, most parishioners subtly moved a few rows away from him. At the end of the service, few members of the church spoke with the Birdman or even acknowledged him as he stood near the foyer at the back door. Almost all of the parishioners looked down at the ground when walking by the Birdman to avoid making eye contact. This went on for years.

Without question, the Birdman suffered from serious psychological illness, and he was hanging on by a thread to his sanity. The Birdman no longer fit into our society, and even those with the best intentions would not dare engage him in conversation. As a kid, I adopted the conventional practices of the other parishioners and did my best to avoid the Birdman. Then, one summer day, everything changed.

An Eye-Opener for an Eight-Year-Old Boy

While driving home one Sunday morning about a block away from church with my mother, I saw the Birdman from a distance walking on the sidewalk down the street. As our car slowly approached the Birdman, negative thoughts entered my mind about the man who was a pariah in our small town. The thoughts of an eight-year-old were disturbingly negative.

To my horror, my mother slowed our car as we approached the Birdman, and our car pulled up to the side of the road next to him. I had no idea why my mother was stopping. My mother opened the passenger side window and asked the Birdman if he wanted a ride. The Birdman got in the back seat of our car, and my mother drove him to his group home a few blocks away.

A little eight-year-old boy learned a lesson that he would never forget. And I give thanks for this special gift.

Few words were said that day between my mother and the Birdman, but a very simple gesture changed my view of mental illness that day forever. Instead of viewing the Birdman as a despicable man, my mother treated him as a human being worthy of respect and kindness.

A Lesson in Kindness and Compassion

When the Birdman got out of our car that day, he didn't say thank you. Perhaps this simple act of kindness was quickly forgotten by the Birdman, but a little eight-year-old boy learned a lesson that he would never forget.

And I give thanks for this special gift.

* * *

A Life Well Lived

While I was visiting my mother at her condo in Florida, a complete stranger stopped me outside on the beach and gave me a bear hug. Naturally, I thought it was a case of mistaken identity, but it wasn't.

The stranger asked, "You're Sally Fisher's son, right?" When I confirmed the stranger's suspicion, he explained the reason for the bear hug.

Turns out, my mother made frequent visits to this man's severely disabled brother at an institution for the disabled. This man's brother could not speak or move and was severely brain damaged. My mother didn't know this disabled man, but every so often she went to spend time with him (because his family did not live nearby).

Not too long ago, I learned that the disabled man had died. Life could not have been more difficult for this man, but one person, "Saint Sally," made sure that he knew that his life mattered and that she cared.

Saint Sally taught her children—not by her words but by the way she lived her life. And everyone who knows her has been blessed by this special person.

How a Mother's Living Example Changed a Little Boy's Life

You learn from the day-to-day example set by your mother (e.g., her acts of kindness for the homeless, courage at times of intense family struggles, complete selflessness in helping you and your siblings, etc.). The acts of kindness and selflessness shown by your mother were lessons that became permanently ingrained in your brain and will never be forgotten. You will pass these lessons along to your children—not only in the spoken word but also by the life you live.

We do not learn from what people tell us; we learn from how they live their lives. Everything you do—good or bad—sets an example that your children will watch carefully and learn from. Your words mean little, but the way you live your life will be passed onto your children and eventually your children's children.

Thank you, Mom, for living a life of sacrifice and commitment for your children. Reflecting back, I know that your children had the perfect role model.

* * *

What It Means to Be a Hero

A hero is someone who gives their life for you.

A hero is someone who makes incredible sacrifices so you can live a better life.

A hero is someone who pushes you to become the best version of yourself.

A hero is someone who makes you feel like the most important person in the world.

Our heroes are not movie stars or professional athletes.

Our heroes have spent most of their lives with us.

Our heroes are parents—mother, father, or both—who gave everything they had for us.

We would not accomplish anything in this world without our heroes.

Thank you, Mom and Dad, for being my heroes.

GRATITUDE AND LOVE

We can all be successful and make money, but when we die, that ends. But when you are significant is when you help other people be successful. That lasts a lifetime.

—LOU HOLTZ

CHAPTER 27:

WHAT IT MEANS TO BE A FRIEND

This was not your ordinary seventeen-year-old.

Seventeen years old and hanging out with a group of my high school friends at a pub in our hometown, my friend reached into the front pocket of my pants and grabbed my car keys. Not sure what to think, I turned and asked my friend what he was doing. My friend responded, "I'm driving you home." I reassured my friend that I only drank one beer and was fine to drive.

But my friend wouldn't listen and refused to part ways with my keys. It was no longer funny for me. "Give me the keys!" But it was pointless. I could not wrestle the keys away from my friend, and I had no choice. My friend drove me home in his car and dropped me off at my parents' house.

Embarrassed and hoping no one was home, I sneaked into my parents' house and somehow managed to go unnoticed. Later that day, my friend quietly drove my car back to its rightful place in my parents' driveway.

What a Best Friend Is

A true friend does what's right for you—even when you don't want them to. Sure, I was perfectly fine to drive that day, but my friend was taking no chances. My friend only wanted what was best for me, no matter how much I protested. That's what a friend does.

> **A true friend does what's right for you—even when you don't want them to.**

When I look back at that day, I think fondly of my friend—and thank God that I had a friend who only cared about doing what was right for me.

The Best Friend for All of Us

My friend Terence "Terry" Basile died at the age of twenty.

I will never forget Terry because he always made me feel like I was his best friend. Everyone loved Terry—you couldn't resist his charm, and the truth is, Terry had other "best friends." I probably wasn't even in his top ten, but that's OK. In my mind, Terry was the best friend for all of us.

I will never forget that day in the spring of our junior year of high school. And I will never forget a special person who always made me feel like I was his best friend.

May God bless you, Terence Basile. You will always be our best friend.

* * *

How My High School Buddy Changed My Life

Halfway through my junior year of high school, I bumped into my closest friend between classes in the hallway. As we were about to rush on to our next class, I happened to mention to my friend that I had the opportunity to attend a boarding school in my final year of high school. Leaving no doubt or uncertainty, my best friend looked squarely into my eyes and responded without hesitation, "Fish, if I had this chance, I'd do it in a second."

At first, I was surprised by my friend's response. Why would my closest friend want me to leave? But after some thought, I realized that my friend only had one thing in mind: what was best for me. The chance encounter with my friend got me thinking, just maybe boarding school would expose me to new challenges. Facing high-achieving students in boarding school, I would be challenged to become a better student and more independent. Just maybe this wasn't such a bad idea.

How a Year in Exile Changed My Life

After endless interviews at big-name boarding schools, I settled on a boarding school about two hours from home. In our final year of high school, my friends in high school moved on with their lives and I began a year of exile. Boarding school had plenty of negatives, but I was exposed to students who were a lot smarter than me, and I would not have been able to replicate that experience anywhere else. I studied hard, played sports, and eventually graduated from a school where I never felt that I belonged.

But after a year in boarding school, there would be no transition for college. In boarding school, I learned how to budget money and time and live independently from Mom and Dad. I didn't realize it at the time, but a year in boarding school prepared me for college in ways that my beloved high school never could have. In hindsight, I realize that I had a big advantage over the other freshmen in college.

A Chance to Say Thanks

We don't often get a chance to say thank you to our closest friends, but I won't miss this opportunity. My best friend wasn't thinking about what he wanted—he only cared what was best for me. My best friend challenged me to become the best that I could in everything that I did, and it's hard to think where I would be today without his encouragement.

This is the epitome of a best friend: someone who pushes you to achieve things you could not do alone—even when you venture out into strange new places. And I now realize that sometimes it's the quick, spur-of-the-moment conversations with our best friends that can change our lives forever.

Thank you, Matthew J. Nolfo, Esq., for changing my life.

CHAPTER 28:

THE GREATEST DAY OF MY LIFE

It seemed like it was something that could wait. Turns out, it wasn't.

In late December of 2004, my father was dying of cancer. The cancer had taken its toll physically on my dad, and I knew he had only weeks to live. A few months earlier, my dad had expressed the desire to go to a casino in Connecticut, and I promised that I'd take him. Time passed, and my dad's physical condition got worse, but a variety of commitments seemed to get in the way of making the trip.

Upon my return home from work one early winter day, my wife stated in a matter-of-fact tone of voice, "You're taking your dad to the casino on Saturday." I responded that I had other commitments, but I assured my wife that I'd take my dad to the casino when I could find the time. My wife was very firm and left no room for discussion: "You're going on Saturday."

A Day unlike Any Other

That Saturday morning, I arrived at my parent's house at 6:00 a.m. (my dad always wanted to do everything at the crack of dawn.) During our drive to Connecticut, my dad was in obvious pain as he moved from side to side in his seat, but he didn't complain. We spent four hours of father-and-son time, just talking about everything and nothing at all. My dad told funny stories involving some of his clients, and we shared a few laughs and each other's company. I learned things about my father that I had never known.

> I learned things about my father that I had never known.

When we arrived at the casino, my dad pulled up a seat at a blackjack table and gambled for hours. My dad's play of the cards was usually wrong, but we didn't care. My dad and I shared jokes, kidded around, and even won a few hands. We gambled the whole afternoon and into part of the evening. Finally, it was time to leave, but deep down, I don't think either one of us wanted to leave. Around 9:00 p.m., my dad and I started the drive back to New York, and we talked for hours during the drive home.

When we arrived at my parents' house, the clock on the kitchen wall read 1:30 a.m. We had lost track of time—my dad and I had spent almost twenty hours together. My dad was physically wiped out and ready for sleep, and we parted ways in the early morning hours with an embrace. I cherished every moment.

Three weeks later, my dad died at home.

The Best Way to Say Goodbye

When we look back on our lives, we won't think of the stuff we have or the money we've made. We'll think of the special moments that made life worth living. And there was nothing more special than a day spent with my dad just days before his death. When I look back on this day, I know it was the best day of my life.

Some never get to say goodbye to their loved ones. I did more than that—I got a day alone with my dad. And for that special day, I will be forever grateful.

Thank you, Lisa, for a day with Dad that I will always remember.

CONCLUSION:

WHY TODAY MATTERS MOST

In small town America, you hear the same conversations. People talk about their big dreams—namely, what they are going to do "someday." Someday, they will have the perfect job, an amazing marriage, a house on the beach, and a two-hundred-thousand-dollar car. Someday, everything will be perfect. They are convinced that "someday" will come; it's just a matter of when.

"Someday" is nothing more than a fairy tale. Turns out, dreaming of a future utopian state where everything will be perfect is a waste of time. Tomorrow doesn't matter; what matters is today. Even more, what matters most is the present moment you are living in.

It's not the destination that brings joy and fulfillment; it's the journey. Just think about your greatest achievement. When you graduated from college, was graduation day everything you imagined it would be? It was a nice day, but what you recall most were the road trips

> **The journey—not the destination—is what makes life worth living.**

with friends, late night conversations with your best friend, and time just spent hanging out in the dorm. It was the journey that made college a special experience.

Your time is the most special gift you have to offer your friends and family. Give your time to your friends and family freely. When your daughter asks to go for a hike, but you have other plans, change your plans. When your son asks to play catch, but you have work to do, change your plans. Make your children and your spouse the center of your life, and you will be rich.

The journey—not the destination—is what makes life worth living.

If You Die Today

Stephen R. Covey's classic advice was to "begin with the end in mind." Covey urged us to think of the vision for your life *before* you live it. Without a vision for your life—personal and professional—you have no chance of achieving your dreams.

When you die, what goals and dreams do you want to have achieved? You won't achieve your dreams without writing them down. Writing your own obituary is a way to document the vision for your life. Here's my shot.

THE OBITUARY OF JOHN H. FISHER

My life has been blessed by the sacrifices made by my family, friends, and mentors.

John's Final Positive Focus

Every workday, I begin the team meetings at our law firm with a statement of gratitude. When you are grateful, nothing bad can happen. As my final positive focus, I pay tribute to those who made sacrifices to give me a better life.

My mother, Sally A. Fisher. For always making me feel like the most important person in the world. You only saw the good in me.

My father, James H. Fisher, Esq. For being the best role model a lawyer could have. You worked harder than anyone and passed along the most invaluable lesson: hard work beats talent.

My mentors in the practice of law. To John W. Tabner, Esq.; John K. Powers, Esq.; and Daniel R. Santola, Esq., for being the best mentors a lawyer could have. You taught me the skills to run a catastrophic injury law firm. Nothing that I achieved would have been possible without you.

My wife, Lisa M. Fisher. For always believing in me in times of struggle and failure.

My children, Tim, Lily, and Alek Fisher. For making life worth living. You are the joy of my life.

Why John Practiced Law

John loved the practice of law. There is nothing John enjoyed doing more than helping the seriously disabled in medical malpractice and catastrophic injury cases. John was grateful for the opportunity to have a profound impact on the lives of the seriously disabled. That is why John practiced law.

The focus of John's career was helping plaintiffs' lawyers own and operate their own law firms. John's mission was to give plaintiffs' lawyers the resources, knowledge, and practical skills in marketing and management to own and operate their own law firms. To the extent that John helped even one fellow plaintiffs' lawyer become more successful, he fulfilled his mission.

John was the author of best-selling books about law firm marketing and management, including *The Power of a System* and *The Law Firm of Your Dreams*. John's book *The Power of a System* has been named the number-one law firm book of all time. John's books have given lawyers—young and old—the knowledge and resources in marketing and management to create the law firms of their dreams.

John was the founder of a national mastermind for lawyers, Mastermind Experience, in which lawyers across the country collaborate, brainstorm, and share best practices and tips to make their law firms better. John's singular purpose in his professional life was to have the nation's top mastermind for lawyers.

John's Final Wish

You can pay tribute to John's life by paying forward everything you've learned to someone who is less fortunate. By paying forward your gifts, you honor those who have sacrificed for you. When you give without any expectation of getting anything in return, you pave the road for others to succeed. And that is the greatest gift of all.